*"You won't like him.
He's not who you think
he was."*
—A Noted Historian

*"Silver made Tombstone rich.
Wyatt Earp made it famous."*
—JOHN GILCHRIESE

ISBN 0-9639549-4-6

First edition, October 1993
Second printing, September 1994

REVISED & EXPANDED

The Illustrated Life And Times of
Wyatt Earp

BY BOB BOZE BELL

SECOND EDITION

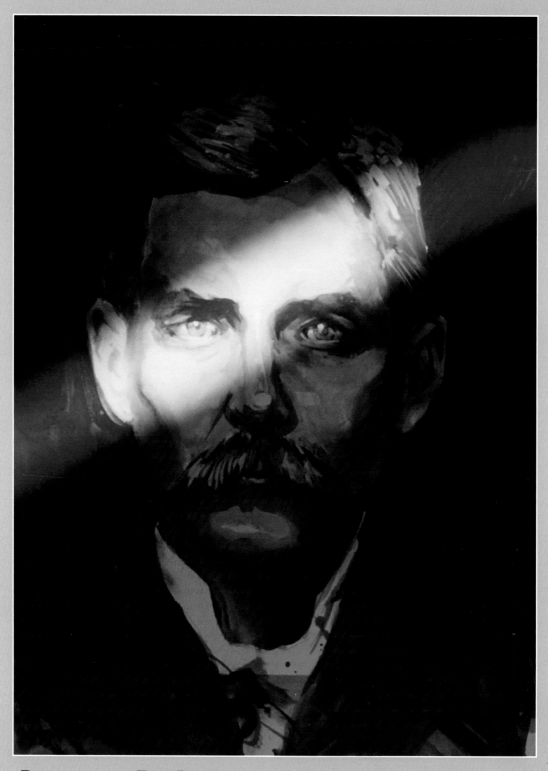

DEAD FROM THE EYES DOWN
"Holliday had few friends anywhere in the west. He was selfish and had a perverse nature—traits not calculated to make a man popular on the frontier."
—Bat Masterson

HEADBANGERS

Bat Masterson and Wyatt Earp in 1877, when they were on the Dodge City police force together. Both became adept at "buffaloeing" malcontents, which involved using a six-shooter as a club and hitting cow-boys upside the head to subdue them. Note the velveteen holsters.

Whether as a successful candidate for Constable of LaMar, Missouri (below), or under arrest for "bunco steering" in Los Angeles (left), the shadow of bars were never far from Wyatt Earp's face.

WHICH SIDE OF
THE BARS DID
HE REALLY
BELONG ON?

W.S. Earp

FOR

CONSTABLE

of

LAMAR
MISSOURI

PART ONE

"It's a boy!"

*Nicholas Earp, 34, and his newborn son, Wyatt Berry Stapp Earp,
ride out the storm.*

HITTING THE GROUND RUNNING

March 19, 1848

Nicholas Earp already has three other sons. His first son, Newton, was born in 1837, but the boy's mother, Abigail Storm Earp, died two years later. Nicholas then married Virginia Ann Cooksley on July 30, 1840 and they produced James and Virgil, both born in Kentucky. After Virgil was born, the family moved to Monmouth, Illinois.

In 1847 Nicholas joined the Illinois Mounted Volunteers to serve under his neighbor, Wyatt Berry Stapp. Nicholas and his unit went to Mexico where 3rd Sergeant Earp was injured and discharged on December 24, 1847.

Today, his fourth son is born, and Nicholas honors him by bestowing upon the lad, the full name of his commanding officer –Wyatt Berry Stapp Earp.

It is raining.

July 19, 1848

A radical, new clothing concept for women, called "Bloomers," is introduced at the first Women's Rights Convention in Seneca Falls, New York.

April, 1849

Nicholas and Virginia Earp move their brood west to Lake Prairie Township, Iowa, where the old man (he's 36) starts a farm and opens a harness repair shop in the town of Pella.

April 24, 1851

Morgan Earp, the fifth son of Nicholas Earp, is born in Pella, Iowa.

March 21, 1852

A tiny baby in Griffin, Georgia is christened. His given name is John Henry Holliday.

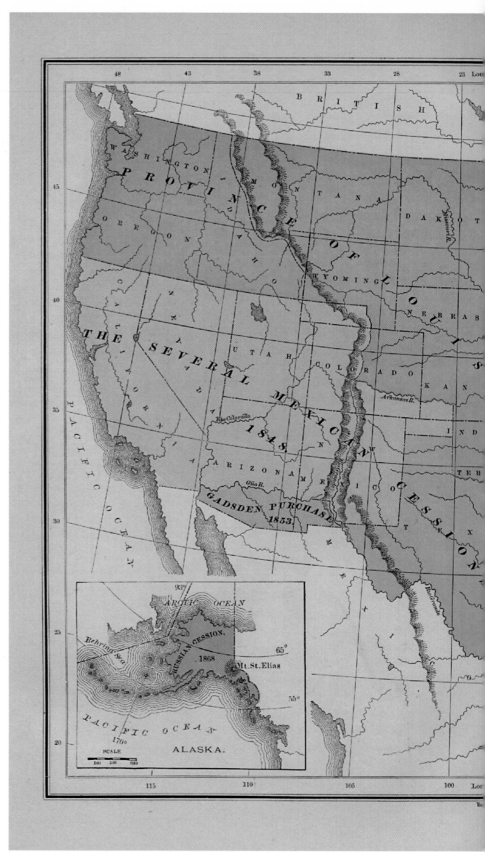

THE NEW WEST IS BORN
While Wyatt is crawling around on the farmhouse floor in Monmouth, Illinois, the United States is giving birth to massive chunks of western territory. He will grow up to roam this vast frontier from end to end.

MAP VII.

SHOWING THE

TERRITORIAL GROWTH

of the

UNITED STATES.

1780 TO 1876.

SCALE OF MILES

March 9, 1855

Warren Earp, the sixth son of Nicholas Earp, is born in Pella, Iowa.

March 22, 1858

Wild Bill Hickok, 20, is elected village constable of Monticello, Kansas.

October 27, 1858

Theodore Roosevelt, Junior is born in the genteel quietness of East Twentieth Street in New York City. He weighs eight and a half pounds naked and his mother says he is "more than usually noisy."

Late 1850s

Nicholas Earp, itching for something new, sells out his holdings in Pella, and moves his family to LaMar, Missouri, where another branch of the Earps are living.

January, 1860

Missouri doesn't pan out, so Nicholas moves back to Pella, Iowa.

February, 1860

Virgil, Virginia's oldest son, gets a neighbor girl pregnant. Virgil is only seventeen, but Ellen Rysdam is even younger. The two lovers run off and get secretly married using fake names, but when they return and tell her parents, Ellen's father has a cow. He tries to have the marriage annulled, but his daughter won't tell him where they got married and since he doesn't know what name they got married under, his efforts are unsuccessful. Still furious nine months later, the father refuses to allow his son-in-law to even see his newborn daughter.

December 20, 1860

South Carolina secedes from the Union with assurances that other states will follow. Sure enough, Mississippi secedes on January 9, 1861, followed two days later by Florida and

Alabama, then Georgia, Louisiana and finally Texas on February 1.

April 12, 1861

At 4:30 A.M. General Pierre Gustave Toutant Beauregard orders his men to open up on Fort Sumter. A perfect sheet of flame will follow.

Spring, 1861

Although Southern born and raised, Nicholas Earp is stoutly opposed to secession and he enters the service of the Union, with his old rank of 3rd Sergeant He is made provost marshal of Marion County, Iowa and in this capacity he recruits and drills three companies of troops for federal service, including his three oldest sons, whom he sends to the front.

March 4, 1861

The Pony Express turns in its best time, delivering President Lincoln's inauguaral address to California in seven days, seventeen hours. The route covers 1,966 miles.

Nicholas and Virginia Earp have a baby girl. They name her Adelia.

Wyatt, not quite thirteen, is in charge of eighty acres of corn while his father recruits and drills troops. Young Wyatt drafts Morgan, 10, and Warren, 6, to help him.

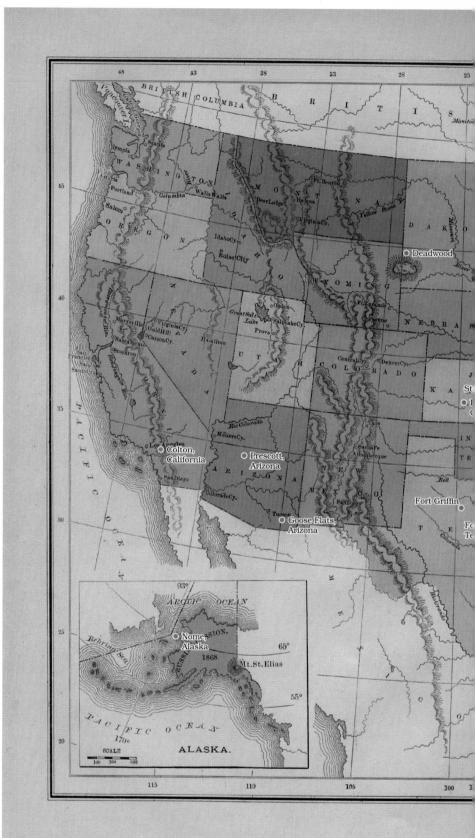

WYATT'S WEST

The Earps were terribly restless and Wyatt carried on the tradition. The above map pinpoints just the early jumping-off points covered in Part One (with the exception of Nome, Alaska which comes later). To cover Wyatt's complete career in the West would take a much larger map.

THE FIGHTING EARPS
Left to right-James, Warren, Wyatt, Nicholas, Virgil and Morgan. Two died from gunshot wounds, four were wounded in gun battles and the father was kicked by a mule. Only one came through it all without a scratch—Wyatt Earp.

"When the Earp boys gather, there is silence, secrecy and clannish solidarity."
—ALLIE EARP

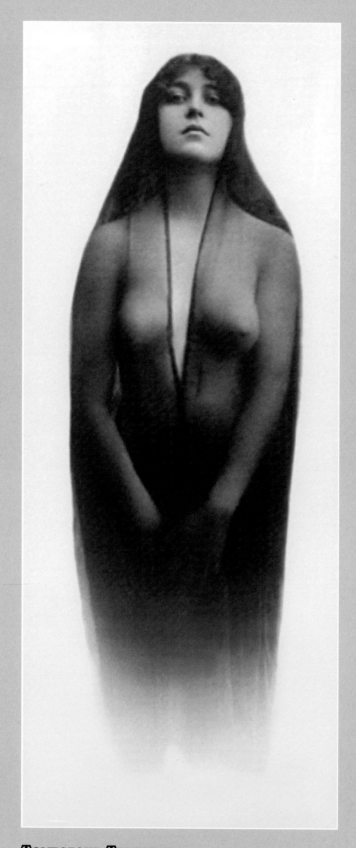

TOMBSTONE TEMPTRESS
A disputed photo of Josephine Sarah Marcus, the actress who stole Wyatt's heart and ruined his second marriage.

May 27, 1862

The Homestead Act becomes law. For a ten-dollar filing fee and a promise to live on the site for five years, a settler may claim up to 160 acres of free public land.

August 21, 1862

Virgil, having become the black sheep of Lake Prairie Township, Iowa, goes back to Monmouth, Illinois and enlists in the 83rd Illinois Infantry.

Wyatt is hoeing the same eighty acres for another crop of corn. While his father is away, the young farmer decides he wants to be like his big brother and runs off to join the army in nearby Ottumwa. About the first person he meets there is his father, who takes him back to the cornfield and makes him promise he will not attempt to enlist without his mother's consent.

January 1, 1863

President Lincoln issues his final Emancipation Proclamation, thereby "freeing the slaves."

Although his sons disagree with him, Nicholas Earp cannot support Lincoln's proclamation.

Abraham Lincoln

He had been a slave-owner himself, and he is sympathetic to the dependence which his Virginia and Kentucky relatives place on the issue. With regret he resigns his army commission and stews about leaving the country.

REDLANDS AND THE SAN BERNARDINO RANGE
This view of Redlands taken about 1915 shows the area where the Nicholas Earps first settled in California. In 1880 they moved to Colton where they remained for the rest of their lives.

February 24, 1863

Arizona becomes a United States territory, formed from half of New Mexico Territory west of the 109th meridian.

Summer, 1863

Serving with Union forces, James Earp receives a severe wound at Fredericktown, Missouri and is sent home to Pella, Iowa as permanently disabled.

Ellen Rysdam, Virgil's child wife, receives word that her husband has been killed in action. Shortly thereafter, she leaves Pella with her family and heads by wagon train towards a new life in Oregon territory.

February 9, 1864

George Armstrong Custer marries Elizabeth Bacon in Monroe, Michigan.

March 19, 1864

Charles Marion Russell is born in Oak Hill, Missouri.

May 12, 1864

Forty wagons and one hundred and fifty emigrants line up at Council Bluffs, Iowa. Nicholas "Captain" Earp leads the caravan across the Missouri River into Omaha, Nebraska and beyond. Sixteen-year-old Wyatt is in charge of the Earp wagons and stock. He also draws the hunter's job and with a gift from his father of an "under-and-over" combination rifle and shotgun he is able to keep a group of twenty people in fresh meat all the way to California.

THE HUNTER
Wyatt is just a teenager on his first wagon train trip, but his father puts the boy in charge of providing meat for the family.

December 19, 1864

Seven months and seven days from Council Bluffs, the Earp wagon train reaches Cajon Pass and drops into the San Bernardino Valley.

Captain Earp has purchased land about twelve miles out of town and the family rolls up their sleeves and prepares to start over.

April 4, 1865

It is Good Friday and today marks the fourth anniversary of the surrender of Fort Sumter. John Wilkes Booth downs two brandies, returns to Ford's Theatre and waits for the laughter to rise. He slips into the president's box, armed with a dagger in his left hand and a derringer in his right. Inches away, Booth fires into the back of Lincoln's head. The bullet tears through the President's brain and lodges behind his right eye. A doctor in the house pronounces the wound mortal.

June 26, 1865

Virgil Earp is mustered out of the army and heads home to see his wife and child.

July 13, 1865

Horace Greeley publishes his famous statement, "Go West, young man, go West," in the New York Times.

"Wyatt Earp was a man of action. He was born, reared and lived in an environment which held words and theories of small account, in which sheer survival often, and eminence invariably, might be achieved through deeds alone."
—STUART LAKE

Horace Greeley

In a related item, Brigham Young takes his 50th bride in Salt Lake City.

Summer, 1865

Seventeen-year-old, Wyatt Earp takes a job driving stage between Los Angeles and San Bernardino. Later in the fall he will go to work for Frank Binkley driving a ten-animal team hauling freight between San Pedro and Prescott, the new capital of Arizona. Fresh out of the army, Virgil is hired by Binkley and joins Wyatt on his long treks. Virgil falls in love with Prescott and vows to live there someday.

Spring, 1866

The budding bullwhacker joins the freight outfit of Chris Taylor, a celebrated frontier wagonmaster. Wyatt, now 18, ramrods a sixteen-animal outfit between San Bernardino and Salt Lake City.

Spring, 1867

Wyatt accepts a partial interest in the freighting outfit of Charles Chrisman, and he moves his freighting activities to Julesberg, Colorado where he drives goods by team to Salt Lake City.

1867

Wild Bill Hickok makes his first dime novel appearance in "Wild Bill the Indian Slayer."

March 4, 1868

The legendary Jesse Chisholm, who blazed the Chisholm Trail, dies of food poisoning at Johnny Left Hand Spring near present-day Geary, Oklahoma. His pards theorize that Chisholm contracted cholera morbus by eating bear's grease which became poisoned by melting it in a brass kettle.

Spring, 1868

Ever restless, Captain Earp decides to visit his old stomping grounds in Illinois. The family travels north by wagon and intercepts the railhead of the Union Pacific Railroad in Wyoming. While there, Wyatt, who has joined them, gets interested in railroad construction and acquires several teams of horses, hires

TEAMSTERS ON THE ROAD
A freight wagon like the ones Virgil and Wyatt manhandled across the Mojave desert, approaches Prescott, Arizona Territory in the 90s.

drivers and goes into the railroad grading business.

It is here, in this environment, that Wyatt, barely 20, finds his true calling when he encounters the whiskey peddlers, whores and gamblers who follow the tracks. He is fascinated by their lifestyle, smart enough to play their games and bold enough to stand up to them.

He also is exposed to one of the most popular sports on the railroad construction sites –boxing. He decides to become a "Sporting Man." A bit of a boxer and a bit of a bettor. Sometimes he competes, sometimes he referees and sometimes he promotes bouts. For Wyatt, fisticuffs, wagering and cards will become a lifetime passion.

February 2, 1870

The territory of Utah, following Wyoming's lead, becomes the second state to grant women the right to vote.

November 8, 1870

Nicholas has moved again. This time he uproots his family and returns once more to LaMar, Missouri. Wyatt returns with the family

Hildreth

[while] he led the other, and [Earp and Kennedy] told him to ride 50 miles towards Kansas...I went with these two men [in a wagon]...on meeting my husband they took the two horses out of the hack and put in the two that [John Shown] had. Earp drove on toward Kansas for three full nights...about 3 o'clock of the 3rd night James M. Keys [the owner of the horses] overtook us. My husband John Shown said [Keys] could have the horses...Earp and Kennedy told Keys that my husband stole the horses. They also said that if Shown (my husband) turned states evidence then they would kill him.

Anna Shown signs her statement with an X.

Bail is set at $500 each. Someone pays Wyatt's bail.

THE RED DECADE

April 15, 1871
Wild Bill Hickok is appointed marshal of Abilene, Kansas. His salary is $150 a week.

May 15, 1871
The Grand Jury at Fort Smith brings in it's first indictments charging sixteen persons with major offenses. Wyatt Earp, along with Ed Kennedy and John Shown, is on the list for horse stealing.

June 5, 1871
Ed Kennedy is put on trial and acquitted of stealing Mr. Keys' horses.

November 21, 1871
The Western District of Arkansas is informed that Wyatt Earp and John Shown cannot be found.

January 31, 1872
Pearl Zane Gray is born in Zanesville, Ohio. He will later drop the first name and change the spelling of the last name after a fan writes, "Dear Miss Grey."

to take up farming. He runs for constable in LaMar, against his half-brother Newton. Wyatt wins the election by 35 votes. Evidently, Wyatt is also plowing more than fields. He rather quickly marries Urilla Southerland (age 21). The bride's family is about as thrilled as Virgil's in-laws were in Iowa. They are even less thrilled when Urilla dies in childbirth. [In 1954, Earp family members will recall that after her death, "Wyatt, Virg, Morgan and James had a 20-minute street-fight with her 2 brothers, Fred and Bert Sutherland and 3 Brummet boys, Granville, Loyd and Garden." The inference being that Urilla's family blamed Wyatt

for her death.]

March 28, 1871
Perhaps still distraught over the death of his wife and baby, young Wyatt has fallen in with a rough crowd. He is indicted in Van Buren, Arkansas, along with two other men (Ed Kennedy and John Shown) for stealing two horses. The alleged theft took place in Indian Territory (Oklahoma) and the owner of the horses is Indian. The details are vague, but according to the indian wife of one of the accused, Wyatt S. Earp and Ed Kennedy "got my husband drunk near Fort Gibson...they went and got Mr. Jim Keys' horses and put my husband on one

BORDERLINE HUMOR

Dodge City and Tombstone had their fair share of wit and humor.

A Tombstone lawyer is pleading his case to a jury in Judge Wells Spicer's court, when a burro beneath the window starts braying loudly. Lawyer Marcus A. Smith, later a United States Senator from Arizona, arises gravely. "If it please the court," he says, "I object to the two attorneys speaking at the same time."

One of the wealthy mining investors ships a Mexican "burro" to his home in Philadelphia for his small son to ride. The animal is billed as a "burro," but the shipping clerk in Philadelphia, never having heard the Spanish term, thinks a mistake has been made and turns in this report: "One bureau short, one jackass over."

A sixty-one round, bare-knuckles prize fight in the Saratoga saloon in Dodge City produced this summary of the fight in the *Dodge City Times* in June, 1877: "The only injuries sustained by the loser in this fight were two ears chewed off, one eye bursted and the other disabled, right cheek bone caved in, bridge of the nose broken, seven teeth knocked out, one jaw bone mashed, one side of the tongue chewed off, and several other unimportant fractures and bruises."

"NOTHING ELSE TO DO."
ONE SOUTHERN GENTLEMAN TO ANOTHER. "Things are very dull. Let's have a shooting match."

GOOD MARKSMANSHIP
Tourist (in Dakota)—"How's the shooting about here—good?"
Native— "Good? Why, it's so well-nigh puffict thet we've had ter build three additions to our cemetery in a year 'n a half."

1872

Wyatt tries buffalo hunting. While camped on the Salt Fork of the Arkansas River, he meets a younger hunter and they hit it off immediately. Bat Masterson invites Wyatt Earp to join his hunting party, which is set to make a sweep through the Texas panhandle. Wyatt declines the offer and heads for Wichita, Kansas, which is becoming the major shipping point for Texas trail herds.

July 16, 1873

The University of California at Berkeley is founded.

July 21, 1873

The world's first train robbery is pulled off by Jesse James and his gang. The notorious outlaw holds up the Rock Island Express and escapes with $3,000.

August 1, 1873

The first cable-car trip is made in San Francisco.

May, 1874

Bessie Earp, "a very beautiful brunette," and wife of James, is charged with prostitution in Wichita, Kansas. She pays the $8 fine and $2 costs. This remains a monthly ritual through March of 1875.

June 3, 1874

Bessie Earp and one "Sallie Earp" are arrested in Wichita and jailed for keeping a "bawdy house" on Douglas Avenue near the Arkansas River bridge.

June 8, 1874

Cochise, the Chiricahua Apache leader, dies of cancer in his Dragoon Mountain stronghold. The site of his burial is never revealed to non-Apaches.

June 27, 1874

In the Texas panhandle, a group of buffalo hunters, including Bat Masterson, holds off a charge of 700 Comanche, Kiowa and Cheyenne warriors, led by Chief Quanah Parker and Lone Wolf. This three-day siege—becomes known as "The Battle of Adobe Walls," named for the crumbling structure the hunters took refuge in.

October 28, 1874

M.R. Mosier of Wichita gets "two officers, John Behrens and Wyatt Earp, to light out upon the trail" of an outfit that left town without paying for a wagon. "These boys fear nothing and fear nobody," the *Wichita Eagle* reports. "They made about seventy-five miles from sun to sun, across trackless prairies, striking the property and the thieves near the Indian line. To make a long and exciting story short, they just leveled a shotgun and a six-shooter upon the scallywags as they lay concealed in some brush, and told them to 'dough over,' which they did to the amount of $146, one of them remarking that he was not going to die for the price of a wagon. It is amusing to hear Mosier tell how slick the boys did the work."

April 21, 1875

Wyatt Earp is officially hired as a policeman in Wichita, Kansas.

May 12, 1875

While officer Earp is questioning a suspected horse thief by the light of the lamp in a Wichita saloon, the suspect breaks and runs. According to the *Weekly Beacon*, Wyatt "fired one shot across his poop deck to bring him to, to use a naughty-cal phrase and just as he did so, the man cast anchor near a clothes line, hauled down his colors and surrendered without firing a gun."

December 8, 1875

Officer Wyatt Earp finds a passed-out drunk lying near the town bridge. As Wyatt takes him to the "cooler" he finds $500 on his person. The *Weekly Beacon* on December 15, beams with pride that Wyatt did not clean him out, and that the "little man" went on his way rejoicing. He may congratulate himself that his lines, while he was drunk, were cast in such a pleasant place as Wichita as there are but few places where that $500 roll would have been heard from. The integrity of our police force has never been seriously questioned. [Maybe their integrity has never been questioned, but perhaps a course in gun safety is in order?]

January 12, 1876

The *Weekly Beacon* reports that last Sunday "policeman Earp was sitting with two or three others in the back room of the Custom House Saloon, his revolver slipped from his holster, and falling to the floor, the hammer which was resting on the cap, is suppose to have struck the chair, causing a discharge of one of the barrels. The ball passed through his coat, struck the north wall and then glanced off and passed through the ceiling. It was a narrow escape and the occurrence got up a lively stampede from the room."

January 24, 1876

Molly Brenan is killed in a Mobeetie, Texas saloon by a stray bullet fired by one of the two men who are fighting over her. Suitor Melvin A. King dies of his wounds suffered at the hands of rival suitor Bat Masterson. Bat is also wounded and will walk with a cane for the rest of his life.

February 1, 1876

Sitting Bull is turned over to the War Department "For such action...as you may deem proper under the circumstances."

April 2, 1876

Wyatt Earp gets in a fist fight with a candidate running for his boss' job. William Smith, who is running against Mike Meagher, allegedly made comments to the effect that City Marshal Meagher was planning to send for Earp's brothers and put them on the

HAM BELL'S VARIETIES, 1870s
The interior of Dodge City's premier dance hall on a slow day. Beyond the monte and faro tables, six couples prepare to "indulge in the giddy dance," and at the far end of the building, a small, raised platform holds the band.

"Fast men and fast women are around by the score, seeking whom they may devour...and many is the Texas cow-boy who can testify as to their ability."
—CORPUS CHRISTI
GAZETTE

force. When it comes to his brothers, Wyatt can be touchy. The *Weekly Beacon* reports that Wyatt "had fight on the brain." and that the city is "properly vindicated in the fining and dismissal" of Earp. Ironically, Mike Meagher wins the election.

April 19, 1876
A Wichita commission votes against rehiring policeman Wyatt Earp. The vote is four in favor and four against—no majority

May 18, 1876
Wyatt is hired and put on the police force at Dodge City, Kansas. He serves under Marshal Larry Deger. A month later, Wyatt and Bat Masterson are deputy sheriffs serving under Ed O. Hougue, and Charlie Bassett, sheriff.

June 4, 1876
A train billed as the "Transcontinental Express" arrives in San Francisco after high-balling it from New York in just over 83 hours.

June 25, 1876
Lt. Col. George Armstrong Custer and 187 of his men are wiped out at the Battle of the Little Big Horn. Unaware that their husbands have been killed this same day, the wives of the 7th Cavalry meet at Fort Lincoln. The prayer meeting is conducted by Mrs. Libby Custer.

July 1, 1876
Wyatt arrests his own boss, Sheriff Ed Hougue for "fighting and disturbing the peace and quiet of the City of Dodge City." Hougue leaves town shortly after this.

August 2, 1876
Wild Bill Hickok is killed while playing poker in Deadwood, Dakota Territory.

WYATT AND WILD BILL

During his lifetime, Wild Bill Hickok was a major Western celebrity. Compared to Earp, Hickok was in another league. Wyatt never once had a dime novel story written about him, while Wild Bill had his own line of stories. Late in life, Wyatt tried to claim that he learned about gun fighting from Hickok personally in Kansas City in the spring and summer of 1871. There is only one problem—Wild Bill wasn't there at that time. The irony is that a century later, both men are equals in the pantheon of Western gunfighters.

Dodge City's Front Street around 1880.

February 16, 1877

The first train chugs into Texas.

February 25, 1877

Levi Strauss is sitting around a campfire wearing his patented, original 501 jeans, which feature, among other places, a rivet at the base of the crotch. After warming himself for about forty-five minutes, the president of the Levis Company starts to get up. He immediately comes in contact with the "hot rivet syndrome" and the offending rivet is banished forever at the next board meeting.

March, 1877

A scouting party under Dan O'Leary heads out from Fort Whipple, Arizona Territory with troops to establish Camp Huachuca near the Mexican border. One of the scouts is 29-year-old Ed Schieffelin.

May 6, 1877

Sioux War Chief Crazy Horse surrenders. U.S. soldiers confiscate 1,700 ponies and 117 rifles from his warriors.

May 8, 1877

After wintering in Pease, Kansas (and finding religion, but then losing it), Mr. and Mrs. Nicholas Earp, Virgil and Allie Earp, and Mr. and Mrs. Newton Earp, head for California via New Mexico and Arizona. The wagon train reaches Prescott, Arizona by the fourth of July, 1877, but Virgil and Allie have dropped off at a ranch in the Verde Valley, where Allie has been offered a job as a midwife. Virgil gets a job driving mail to Prescott.

Nicholas and Virginia proceed on to California where they establish a family headquarters in Colton.

Spring, 1877

Wyatt and Morgan travel north to the booming town of Deadwood, Dakota Territory. Wyatt starts up a wood hauling business. He claims to be making $120 to $130 a day.

While he's in the Dakotas, the Cheyenne and Black Hills Stage and Express Company hires Wyatt to help guard a spring "clean up" of the surrounding gold mines.

Wyatt and the other "special shotgun messengers" deliver the approximately $200,000 shipment in gold through to Cheyenne, Wyoming without mishap.

Summer, 1877

The mayor of Dodge City, James "Dog" Kelley, likes to hunt. In fact, he got his nickname while taking care of Col. Custer's pack of greyhounds. The *Times* reports on a recent deer hunting trek: "They rode fifty miles, let a deer escape (Hungerford's fault) crossed and recrossed the river seven times, chased a herd of antelope four miles, caught 00, struck a skunk's nest, killed 8 and came home highly perfumed."

"The real story of the Old West can never be told, unless Wyatt Earp will tell what he knows; and Wyatt will not talk."
—BAT MASTERSON

WILLIAM BARCLAY "BAT" MASTERSON

July 7, 1877

The *Dodge City Times* notes: "Wyatt Earp, who was on our police force last summer, is in town again. We hope he will accept a position on the force once more. He had a quiet way of taking the most desperate characters into custody which invariably gave one the impression that the city was able to enforce or mandate and preserve her dignity. It wasn't considered policy to draw a gun on Wyatt unless you got the drop and meant to burn powder without any preliminary talk."

September, 1877

Ed Schieffelin records his first claims in the Pima County Courthouse. His first claim he calls the "Toomstone."

November 6, 1877

The polls have closed in Dodge City and the new sheriff of Ford County is Bat Masterson. He wins over Larry Deger by a margin of three votes.

Wyatt travels to Fort Giffin, Texas for a gambling sojourn. He meets Doc Holliday and his volatile consort, Big Nosed Kate for the first time.

January, 1878

Wyatt goes to Fort Worth, Texas. He tries to get an appointment as constable or deputy, but he is unsuccessful.

January 28, 1878

Sheriff Bat Masterson and his posse capture outlaw "Dirty Dave" Rudabaugh, 24 hours after his gang robs a pay train near Kinsley, Kansas.

February 16, 1878

The silver dollar is legalized, making silver a hot commodity.

February, 1878

In Arizona, Ed Schieffelin and Richard Gird return to the "Tombstone" district and locate the "Graveyard" mine. They also discover a lode that assays $15,000 to the ton and

*Ed Schieffelin, the "lucky cuss" who found more than his tombstone out
on the San Pedro. According to Allie Earp his hair was flaming red.*

immediately name the mine "The Lucky Cuss".

April 9, 1878

Marshal Ed Masterson, Bat's older brother, is shot dead by a drunk cow-boy outside the Lady Gay Dance Hall in Dodge City, Kansas.

April, 1878

As word leaks out, miners and adventurers begin to converge on Goose Flats, Arizona Territory, staking claims right and left.

Working against the clock, Ed Schieffelin and Richard Gird discover two more veins and name them the "Toughnut," and the "Contention."

May 8, 1878

Wyatt returns from Fort Worth, Texas and is appointed Assistant Marshal of Dodge City. His salary is $75 dollars a month. He has brought a woman with him. Her name is Celia Ann Blaylock, but Wyatt calls her "Mattie," and they appear to be married. The bride and groom are just in time for a cattle season that will break all previous records in Dodge for numbers of cattle shipped—and for blood spilled.

June, 1878

Anson P.K. Safford, third territorial governor of Arizona, begins investing in the Tombstone area.

June 5, 1878

Doroteo Arango is born in San Juan del Rio, Mexico. He will later become known as "Pancho" Villa.

June 18, 1878

The Globe reports that: "Wyatt Earp is doing his duty as Ass't Marshal in a very creditable manner—adding new laurels to his splendid record every day."

July 26, 1878

Three Texas cow-boys decide to "hurrah" Dodge City before they ride back to camp. It's three

A PLAGUE OF TEXANS
Wyatt will get his share of Texans in his life. Many, like these cow-boys who work for Texas John Slaughter saw Earp in Kansas and in Arizona.

o'clock in the morning as they mount up and "commence to bang away." One of their stray bullets whizzes into a dance hall where Eddie Foy, nationally known actor and comedian, is watching Bat Masterson dealing in a game of Spanish monte with Doc Holliday. After the shots, Foy is impressed with the "instantaneous manner in which they flattened out like pancakes on the floor." Policemen Wyatt Earp and Jim Masterson mount up and give chase, sending "two or three volleys" after the fleeing cow-boys. As the herders ride across the bridge followed by the officers, one of the cow-boys falls from his horse. His name is George Hoy and he has been hit in the arm by the officer's fire. He will live not quite a month but the enmity and friction between Dodge

City lawmen and Texas cattlemen will live on considerably longer.

August, 1878

The Republicans of Ford County, Kansas meet to choose their delegates to the Kansas State Republican convention to be held in Topeka on August 28. Wyatt Earp helps choose the delegates.

August 17, 1878

Wyatt, along with Jim Masterson, gets in some aerobic exercise. The two lawmen attempt to calm an "intoxicated and troublesome cow-boy" in the Comique Theatre. The bystanders, all Texas cattlemen, come to the cow-boy's aid and join in the fight. Wyatt and Jim have to bruise a few Texas heads with their six-shooters to break free. Several shots are fired but no one is injured. The Globe is not very appreciative of the officer efforts: "We...cannot help but regret the too ready use of pistols in all rows of such character and would like to see a greater spirit of harmony exist between our officers and cattlemen..."

Researchers speculate that this may have been the time when Doc Holliday saved Wyatt's life.

September 26, 1878

The Dodge City newspapers report that "No less than half a dozen shooting scrapes occurred in our city during the past week."

October 4, 1878

The son of a wealthy Texas cattleman fires four shots into Mayor "Dog" Kelley's house in retaliation for rude treatment in hizzoner's saloon. The mayor is not home, but one of the forty-five calibre bullets goes through the front door, passes through Fannie Garrettson's bedclothes (she's sleeping in the mayor's bed), through the plaster partition separating the two bedrooms, striking Dora Hand, a house guest, and killing her instantly.

October 5, 1878

A well armed group of lawmen sets out from Dodge City to catch the killer of Dora Hand. The hard-riding posse includes Sheriff Bat Masterson, Marshal Charlie Bassett, Assistant Marshal Wyatt Earp, Deputy Sheriff William Duffy, and Bill Tilghman (certainly one of the most legendary posses ever assembled.)

Guessing at James Kennedy's escape route, the posse, after a 75-mile, all-night ride, actually gets ahead of the fleeing killer in a rain storm and waits for him at a ranch near Meade, Kansas.

Riding into the trap, the fleeing suspect is "thrice commanded... to throw up his hands." Kennedy makes a move to quirt his horse and in a withering barrage, the officers bring down

COWTOWN COMIC

Eddie Foy was an actor, vaudeville player and comedian who played cattle and mining theatres, including Dodge City and Tombstone. His specialty was black-face and Irish comedy. During the four-hour shows, Foy and a female singer named Miss Belle Lamont performed comedy routines together. A sample of their "snappy repartee" is as follows:
Said he: "Belle, you are my dearest duck."
Said she: "Foy, you are trying to stuff me."

GOOSE FLATS GROWS UP

The fledgling town of Tombstone, 1879, begins to blossom off the desert floor of Goose Flats. All tents and cabins, the embryonic community will explode in coming months.

horse and rider.

Suffering from a bad wound in the left shoulder, Kennedy is brought back to Dodge where the Globe describes him as "a cold-blooded assassin" and "a fiend in human form."

A week later, behind closed doors, the cold-blooded assassin is acquitted because of the "evidence being insufficient." The rumor on the streets is that Kennedy's powerful father, who co-founded the famous King ranch in Texas, paid off the officials. Some believe that this event soured Wyatt Earp on "lawing." Others believe he probably received part of the bribe–if there was one. It is just a rumor.

December, 1878

Salon Allis surveys the Tombstone townsite. The principal streets running east and west are named Toughnut, Allen, Fremont and Safford. The streets running north and south are numbered 1 through 28.

There is no water on the mesa so a mill is built on the San Pedro River ten miles southwest of Tombstone. The mill and the tents springing up around it receive the moniker "Charleston."

February 10, 1879

The first electric lights are used in a theatre in San Francisco.

April 12, 1879

Brewer Adolph Coors marries

Louisa M. Weber in Golden, Colorado.

1879

In a Safford, Arizona saloon, Louis Hancock is wounded in the jaw by Johnny Ringo, during a drunken quarrel.

May, 1879

The population of the village of Tombstone is 250. The Tombstone Townsite Company is formed.

May 5, 1879

No doubt fed up with lawing, cow-boys and Kansas, Wyatt almost gets himself killed when he attempts to disarm three unruly Missourians who are

For Sheriff
OF
YAVAPAI
COUNTY

J.H. BEHAN

H.V. CRAM
VARIETY STORE

H.S. STEVENS
FOR CONGRESS

FOR SHERIFF
J.H. BEHAN

PRESCOTT, ARIZONA TERRITORY, 1870S

It's election time in the new capital of Arizona. Hyram S. Stevens is running for the legislature and John H. Behan is running for sheriff of Yavapai County. Both win. Behan has been active in politics since his arrival in Arizona, having served as representative of Mojave and Yavapai Counties. However, Behan trips when he runs for recorder in August of 1880. He is bitter about the defeat, feeling he wasn't adequately backed by his Democrat friends. He will receive a bone in about six months.

Meanwhile, Virgil Earp has been driving a stage to the surrounding mining camps including Tiptop (where Johnny Behan lives), Auga Fria, Gillett, Black Canyon, Humbug, Big Bug, Cottonwoods, Bumblebee and the little village of Phoenix.

THE EARPS BURN BIG MIKE

"Big" Mike Goldwater, (above left) gets ready to go on a picnic with friends in 1880. It was no picnic when customers left without paying for goods and that's what Virgil and Allie allegedly did to Mike. The Goldwater store, (below) was a fixture in Prescott and later became a successful chain.

trying to "take the town." Sheriff Bat Masterson happens on the scene "in the nick of time," according to the *Dodge City Times*, and "using the broad side of his revolver" lays out the shooter before he can inflict Wyatt with "lead poisoning."

All in all however, the '79 cattle season is a tame one. The *Globe* will report that "There have been only two men killed in Dodge this summer, for which we deserve due credit. The police, under Marshal Bassett, are compelled to practice on old oyster cans in order to keep their hands in. The morals of our city are improving. There are only 14 saloons, 2 dance halls, and 47 cyprians [whores] in our metropolis of 700 inhabitants."

September, 1879

Virgil and Allie have since moved into Prescott, where Virgil works in a sawmill and also is a deputy sheriff. Of course, the mining strike at Goose Flats is big news in Prescott and many prospectors and Boomers have already gone south (the very first stage to leave Prescott for the Tombstone mining district is robbed by highwaymen).

Virgil sends word to Wyatt of the boom in Tombstone. With the cattle season over, and morals rapidly improving, Wyatt feels Dodge City has "lost its snap" and writes Virgil back to say "count me in." Within a week, the Dodge City Earps sell out, load up and head out for the Arizona Territory.

November 1, 1879

Several wagons and fifteen head of thoroughbreds reach Prescott, A.T. In the lead wagon is Wyatt and his wife Mattie. Behind them are James and Bessie Earp and her two children, Hattie and Frank Ketchum. John H. "Doc" Holliday is along with his on-again, off-again Kate. Virgil has sold his business interest [there is a local tradition that Virgil also burned the Goldwater Store for $314 in unpaid merchandise] and resigned as deputy sheriff. Virgil and Allie pull their wagon in line and the wagon train heads south towards Crown King and the Tombstone mining district. At the last minute, Doc stays behind, having hit a run at the local faro tables.

November 27, 1879

Stopping off in Tucson, Virgil Earp receives a commission as a Deputy United States Marshal [pay attention, this is important later.]

Wyatt, as you may remember, is tired of lawing and has plans to start a stage line running out of Tombstone.

November, 1879

The sheriff of Pima County, Charles A. Shibell, takes the first official census of Tombstone village. He counts just under 1,000 people.

November 29, 1879

The Earp wagon train arrives in Tombstone "We could see it plain," said Allie, "a hodgepodge of shacks, adobes and tents."

Every house is taken so the Earps rent a one-room adobe on Allen Street. No floor, just hard packed dirt. The price? $40 a month. The family rolls up their sleeves, fixes the roof, drives the wagons up on each side and take the wagon sheets off the bows to stretch out for more room. They cook in the fireplace and use boxes for chairs.

October 2,1879

The first issue of the *Nugget*, Tombstone's first newspaper, rolls off the press.

December 1, 1879

The O.K. Corral is under construction.

The Jacob Brothers of Tucson open the Pima County Agency Bank in Tombstone.

PHOENIX, ARIZONA, 1879.
The sleepy village has a population of slightly more than 150 souls and is two years away from incorporation.

"We went through a little Mexican town called Phoenix where I saw my first beautiful, real Spanish ladies, fair, slender, with big brown eyes, and hair black and shiny as ravens' wings at a house where Mattie and I went for drinking water."
—ALLIE EARP

TOMBSTONE, LOOKING NORTHWEST, 1880

January, 1880

Fred White becomes the first city marshal of Tombstone village.

February, 1880

Tombstone's population now stands at 2,000.

Water is being hauled into town and sells for three cents a gallon.

April, 1880

John Phillip Clum, Thomas R. Sorin and Charles D. Reppy organize a publishing firm known as the "Clarion." Eventually, they decide to change the name to the "Epitaph" and publish the first issue of their newspaper on May 1, 1880.

May, 1880

Wells Fargo establishes an office in Tombstone with Marshall (his name, not his title) Williams as agent.

A fire burns out the Dexter corral due to lack of water and firefighting equipment.

There are 110 Chinese in Tombstone.

There is no jail worthy of the name, no official courthouse, no fire or hose department and no city hall.

WITH FRIENDS LIKE THESE...

Ike Clanton (right) *tries opening a restaurant in Tombstone in the early days of the camp. His efforts are not successful. Perhaps this picture casts some light on why. He is seen here treating his cow-boy friends to a "jollification." (l to r), King Pin, Zwing Hunt, Curly Bill, Ike and Dixie Gray.*

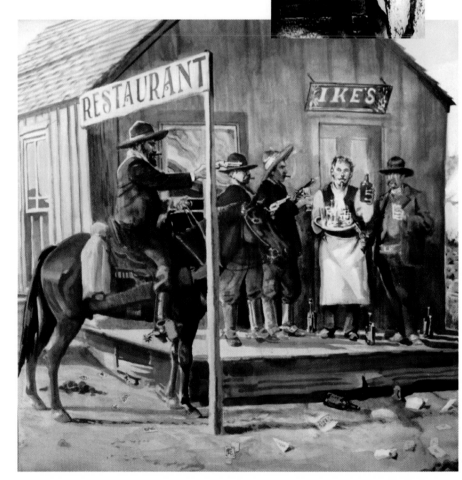

U.S. Marshal Crawley Dake, 1879

As head of the Marshals in Arizona, it is Crawley who gives Virgil his commission before Earp goes to Tombstone. A staunch supporter of the Earps, he will be sued by the federal government for the $3,000 he gives Wyatt to pursue outlaws.

June, 1880

The population of Tombstone has increased to 3,000 people.

The Oriental Saloon and Gambling Parlor opens at Fifth and Allen.

Ike Clanton starts a small restaurant in Tombstone. Mexico provides the beef.

Approximately 20 people a day are now arriving in the camp.

July, 1880

Joe Hill, alias "King Pin," rides into San Carlos, Arizona Territory with $2,000 worth of cattle. With him are Dutch George, Ike Clanton (obviously out procuring beef for his restaurant) and another unknown cow-boy. The four "stock raisers" attempt to unload the cattle on the reservation beef contractor, but he is suspicious of the cattle's origin and will not buy them until he hears from the governing officer in Silver City, New Mexico. Over a barrel, King Pin and his cohorts cave in and the contractor gets the whole herd dirt cheap. Mad as hell, the cow-boys leave San Carlos and head up the Gila towards Safford, shooting into every house they ride by. Once in Safford they shoot out the lamps in Harrison's saloon and a private residence. They open up Franklin's Store and shoot at "everything they fancied." They force Mr. Jacobs to pour out drinks and then they stir their cocktails with the muzzle of their pistols. A bystander is encouraged to dance. The cow-boys finally

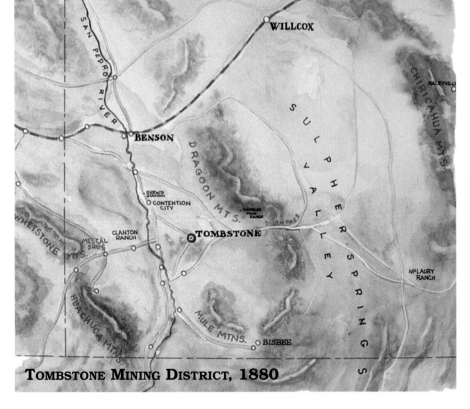

TOMBSTONE MINING DISTRICT, 1880

TOMBSTONE MINING EXCHANGE

retire to Jacob's mill, forcing at gunpoint one of the employees to furnish cartridges so they can have their jolliest time firing fifty shots into the buildings. Tapped out of fresh targets and drunk as skunks, the cow-boys head for Solomon for another "jollification."

July, 1880

Whorehouses are being constructed on Sixth Street faster than you can say, "Lickity Split." There is no "Grand Opening," but the cow-boys and miners line up to "beat the bang."

In addition to the red-light trade, there are four breweries in town, one winery, sixty saloons and sampling houses.

Ninety-five miles to the east of Tombstone, another town is born. Galeyville begins to take the shape of a comer and the cow-boys consider it their town.

July 21, 1880

Six government mules are stolen from Camp John A. Rucker, A.T. (Arizona Territory). The thieves are believed to be Curly Bill, Pony Deal, Zwing Hunt and Sherm McMasters. It is common knowledge that the mules have been secreted at the McLaury's Babocomari ranch until they can be fenced. It is also reported that the US brands on the mules have been changed to D8.

July 22, 1880

The Occidental Saloon opens for business.

Anti-Chinese agitation causes several killings and stabbings.

Tombstone miners form a union and agitate for better wages. They want to go from $2.50 to $3.00 a day.

July 28, 1880

Sheriff Shibell appoints Wyatt Earp Deputy Sheriff for "this precinct."

July 30, 1880

First Lieutenant J. H. Hurst

VIRGIL & ALLIE

They met in 1873 in Council Bluffs Iowa. He was driving a stage and she was waiting tables at the Planters House. Virgil always remembered that when he first laid eyes on her, she was about to take a bite out of a pickle. Years later she related that when she was mean, Virgil would say she was just as sour as that pickle, "but mostly he said I was not much bigger than a pickle but a lot more sweet."

"For any woman, one good man's plenty, and one poor one's too many."
—ALLIE EARP

WYATT UNARMED?

When the Marshal White shooting occurred, Wyatt Earp was in Billy Owen's saloon. He wasn't armed and as he ran to the scene, he tried to borrow a pistol from his brother Morgan. Evidently, Wyatt Earp didn't go heeled everywhere, and the fact that he wasn't armed at night, in a saloon, in Tombstone, is significant.

THE WHITE SHOOTING

"I'm hit," Marshal White said as Curly Bill's revolver went off, striking him in the left testicle.

prints a reward notice in the *Epitaph*, offering $25 for each of the thieves who stole the six government mules from Camp Rucker. In the reward notice, Hurst prominently names Frank McLaury as one of the accomplices.

August 5, 1880

Frank McLaury answers the mule theft charges by publishing his own "card" in the Tombstone weekly *Nugget*. In it McLaury calls First Lt. Hurst a "coward, a vagabond, a rascal and a malicious liar." He goes on to say that "this base and unmanly action is the result of cowardice, for instead of hunting the stock himself he tried to get others to do it [the Earps], and when they could not find it, in order to cover up his own wrong acts, he attempted to traduce the character and reputation of

honest men."

Frank goes on to say, "My name is well known in Arizona and thank God this is the first time in my life that the name of dishonesty was ever attached to me."

"I think thou dost protest too much."
  —William
    Shakespeare

September, 1880

 Camillus S. Fly builds a photography studio behind his boarding house on the south side of Fremont near Third Street.

September 10, 1880

In Tombstone's very first election, Alder Randall is elected Mayor, Fred White is marshal, S.W. Dyer is assessor, J.C. Kennedy is pound master.

September, 1880

George E. Goodfellow resigns from the United States Army and appears in Tombstone determined to open a hospital.

The Sycamore Water Company begins to furnish Tombstone with its first regular water, piped in from Sycamore Springs near the Dragoon Mountains.

October 28, 1880

Virgil Earp is appointed assistant marshal of the village with a salary of $100 a month.

About 12:30 in the morning, three or four pistol shots are heard in Tombstone. Wyatt Earp is in Billy Owen's saloon and he runs outside at the sound of the first shot. As he does, he sees the flash of a pistol up the street about a block away. As he starts to run towards the shooting in the dark, he hears the report of several more shots, fired in quick succession. When Wyatt gets to the scene, he meets his brother, Morgan, and Fred Dodge who

DOC HOLLIDAY IN PRESCOTT, 1879
When the Wyatt Earp wagon train came through Prescott to pick up Virgil and Allie, Doc was with them. When they all departed for Tombstone, Doc stayed behind and shows up on the 1880 census. He evidently had this photo taken while he enjoyed the mile-high city.

BUCKSKIN FRANK LESLIE, 1880
When the Mining Journal *came to Tombstone to do an entire issue on the booming camp, they chose Buckskin Frank as the feature "personality." Wyatt Earp is not mentioned.*

"To kill your man seems a way of winning your spurs, as it were, and establishing yourself on a proper footing in the community."
—WILLIAM HENRY BISHOP

have run down from Vogan's saloon. Both Morgan and Fred are crouching by a chimney outside of their cabin, between Allen and Toughnut, on Fifth. A half-dozen cow-boys appear to be shooting from an arroyo just below the cabin. Wyatt is unarmed and asks Morgan for a pistol, but he won't give it to Wyatt because he may need it. Fred Dodge gives Wyatt his revolver, and as stray bullets ricochet off the chimney, Wyatt runs forward into the fray. Just as he approaches the knot of shooters, he hears someone say, "I am an officer, give me your pistol." In the black confusion, Wyatt recognizes Marshal Fred White's voice and quickly throws his arms around the cow-boy White is grappling with. As Wyatt does so, Fred White says, "Now you God-damn son of a bitch, give up that pistol," as he gives a quick jerk to the cow-boy's weapon.

There is an explosion as the gun goes off, striking White above the left testicle. The intimate proximity of the powder flash sets his pants on fire and as he falls, White says, "I am shot."

Wyatt strikes the assailant over the head with Dodge's pistol which sends the cow-boy crashing after White. Morgan and Dodge run up and Wyatt tells them to put out the fire in Marshal White's pants. Wyatt picks up the cow-boy's pistol, grabs him by the collar and tells him to get up. The defendant is indignant, and demands, "What have I done? I have not done anything to be arrested for."

Wyatt will testify later that he did not notice if the defendant was drunk.

During the shooting and melee, the other cow-boys scatter into the darkness. As Marshal White is quickly carried to a doctor, Wyatt and Virgil start rounding up the shooters and put them in the 10' x 12' wooden plank jail, which is literally a stone's throw from the shooting. A deadline is established around the small jail

BILLY CLANTON, AGE 18

and Morgan and Fred Dodge stand guard inside it as Virgil and Wyatt, and several others start bringing in cow-boys until the tiny calaboose can't hold any more.

A couple of the cow-boys are feared to have escaped the roundup in the confusion and there is a very real fear that they will return with reinforcements.

The Earps and Dodge stand guard all night, but no attempt is made to spring the prisoners.

In the morning, Wyatt Earp brings the prisoner before Judge Gray on a warrant charging him with assault to murder. The defendant gives his name as William Rosciotis and claims to hail from the San Simon country. His real name is William Brocius, alias Curly Bill.

October 29, 1880

Marshal White is resting. His wound, while quite painful, is not expected to be life-threatening. When he awakens, he gives a statement, under oath, in which he exonerates Curly Bill and says the shooting was an accident.

A rumor circulates that Marshal White will not live until sundown and that a Vigilance committee is organizing a necktie party.

A buggy is brought up to the

BILLY BREAKENRIDGE, 1880
Hailing from Watertown, New York, "Breck" as his friends called him, first settled in the Salt River Valley where he engaged in freighting and farming. In 1877 he was made County Surveyor of Maricopa County and the following year he became a deputy under Sheriff Thomas. In the fall of 1880 he came to the Tombstone Mining District as a prospector and was made a deputy by Johnny Behan.

Gunplay?

Parsons: "While working in Ecclestons today Walter jerked his big Colt's playfully calling my attention to it and deliberately pulled the trigger sending the ball to one side of me into some hardware, only injuring an auger...am getting pretty well used to bullets."

WHAT THINGS COST

A "good" meal is fifty cents.

A hundred pounds of flour is $6.

A pound of potatoes is four cents.

A pound of bacon is twenty cents.

A pound of ham is 16 to 20 cents.

A pound of steak is eight to fifteen cents.

A gallon of whiskey is $2 to $8.

A gallon of mescal is $4 .

A dozen home-made beers are $3.

A dozen imported beers are $5. (Coors would be imported—from Colorado.)

A gallon of turpentine is $2.

A steel hammer is 35 to 50 cents.

A keg of nails is $14.

A keg of horse shoes is $14.

A dozen axes are $15 to $24.

A good wool mattress is $6.

A pillow costs $1.

A wooden chair costs $1.

A plain table costs $6.

A lamp costs $6.

A curtain costs $1.25.

A pen rack costs $1.

A journal and ledger costs $2.

A basin and glass costs $1.

A shanty that cost $50 to build rents for $15 a month.

A lot 30 by 80 feet, on Allen Street, between Fourth and Sixth, is worth $6,000.

A dozen eggs cost seventy-five cents.

A yard of calico costs twenty-five cents.

A pair of dusters can be had "on sale" at the San Jose House for twenty-five cents.

jail and Wyatt Earp takes the reins as Curly Bill is spirited into the outgoing hack. Curly Bill and Wyatt, accompanied by George "Shotgun" Collins, head for Tucson at a trot. They are surrounded by a well-armed entourage that includes Virgil and Morgan Earp, who follow until the buggy is several miles out of town.

October 30, 1889
Saturday morning, Marshal White's condition worsens and he dies.

Ben Sippy is appointed marshal to replace White.

November 15, 1880
Virgil Earp resigns as assistant marshal.

November 29, 1880
Buckskin Frank Leslie is granted power to arrest people on the premises of the Oriental Saloon.

December, 1880
Wyatt Earp is out scouting water rights on the east slope of the Huachuca mountains. While returning from the Huachucas, Wyatt meets Sherm McMasters on the road, who tells Earp that if he hurries he will find his missing horse, Dick Nailer (which is a nasty play on words—"Dick nail her"), in Charleston. As Wyatt rides in he sees his horse going through the streets to the corral. He puts up for the night in another corral and goes to the local judge's office to get papers for the recovery of his horse. But the judge is not home—having gone down to Sonora to some coal fields that had recently been discovered. Wyatt then telegraphs Tombstone with instructions for his brother Warren to get papers made out and delivered to him in Charleston as soon as possible. While Wyatt is waiting for them to be delivered, Billy Clanton finds out that Earp is in town and tries to take the stolen horse out of the corral, but Wyatt goes down and

THE GUNFIGHTERS

Class of '81

Among the notable fighting men whose exploits sent Tombstone's fame "swirling to the frontier skies in clouds of six-shooter smoke."

Buckskin Frank Leslie
Luke Short
Peter Spencer
Johnny Ringo
Tom Horn
Billy Grounds
Frederick Burnham
Russian Bill
Jaw Bone Clark
Chacon
Three Fingered Jack
Billy Stiles
Texas John Slaughter
Black Jack Ketchum
George "Shotgun" Collins
Bob Paul
Bat Masterson
James Hume
Texas Jack Vermillion
Turkey Creek Johnson
Coyote Smith
Ike Clanton
Finn Clanton
Billy Clanton
Old Man Clanton
Joe Hill
Sherman McMasters
Hank Snelling
Crawley Dake
Doc Holliday
Charlie Storms
Wyatt Earp

OLD MAN CLANTON

JOHNNY RINGO

CURLY BILL

TOM McLAURY

PETE SPENCE

IKE CLANTON

FLORENTINO

GERONIMO MIRANDA

CHACON

FRANK McLAURY

ZWING HUNT

BILLY THE KID CLAIBORNE

TEXAS JOHN SLAUGHTER

PONY DEAL

THE COW-BOY CROWD

Ranging from the San Simon to the Mexican border, these men were part of a looseknit fraternity of "stockmen" who weren't afraid of using their weapons to protect their territory against encroachment from outsiders—which, to them, included Indians, Mexicans, the federal government and the Earps.

physically stops him. But the nineteen-year-old Clanton is feisty and won't back down. He refuses to give "his" horse to a stranger who doesn't even have any papers. The tense standoff continues until Warren shows up, having ridden like the wind from Tombstone. Finally sensing defeat, Billy quickly gives up the horse without being served and sarcastically asks Wyatt if he has "any more horses to lose." Wyatt leads his horse out of the corral and replies that he will keep all of his horses in the stable after this and give Billy Clanton no chance to steal them.

December, 1880

Construction begins on Schieffelin Hall on the northeast corner of Fourth Street and Fremont.

The federal census now lists the inhabitants of Tombstone as numbering 5,300.

January 4, 1881

John Philip Clum is elected mayor of Tombstone, receiving 532 votes.

Curly Bill and his gang shoot their guns off in the Alhambra Saloon and race their horses recklessly down Allen Street, "hurrahing" the town.

John H. Behan of Prescott, Arizona is appointed Deputy Sheriff of Pima County for the Tombstone district, replacing Wyatt Earp.

January 14, 1881

W.P. Schneider, chief engineer of the Corbin Mill in Charleston, is taking his lunch break at a nearby restaurant. [This much everyone agrees with. The *Epitaph* of the following day, no doubt quoting friends of Schneider's, prints the following version of events]

"Upon entering, Mr. Schneider approaches the stove to warm himself. After thawing out for a few moments, Mr. Schneider comments to a nearby friend that

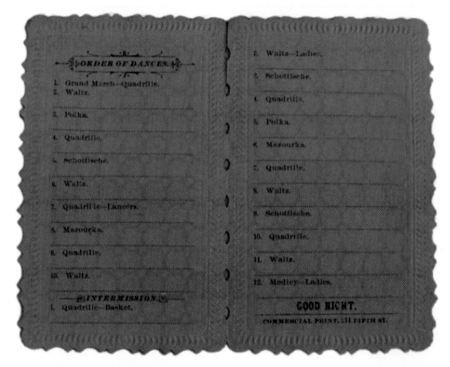

SAVE THE LAST DANCE FOR ME

An actual 1881 dance card from Tombstone. At the time, the waltz was a relatively new dance and considered quite scandalous back east—"My God, the man and woman actually touch!" Naturally, Westerners loved it. Notice who is on the Arrangements Committee—G.F. Spangenberg, owner of the gun shop. And the mayor, John Clum is on the Reception Committee. By the way, what the hell is a dance called the Mazourka?

WOODEN WYATT
Like many men of action, Wyatt Earp (above) was a clumsy, stiff dancer. Johnny Behan on the other hand was a very good dancer and in fact traveled to San Francisco once for lessons—it was on that trip that he met Sarah Marcus (right). Wyatt obviously didn't let the handicap slow him down as you can see from the above photo that he's not dancing with his wife.

it was warm inside the engine room of the mine but he got a bad chill when he stepped out into the cold air. A local gambler named Johnny-Behind-the-Deuce is sitting nearby and he pipes off sarcastically, 'I thought you never got cold.'

"Not desiring to have anything to do with one of Mr. Deuce's character, Mr. Schneider turns and coldly says, 'I was not talking to you.'

"This raises the lurking devil in the diminutive heart of Johnny-Behind-the-Deuce and he blurts out, 'God-damned you, I'll shoot you when you come out!'" And with that, Mr. Behind stomps out of the eating house.

After eating, Mr. Schneider passes out the door and is proceeding to the mill when he is dropped in his tracks by a deadly shot from ambush.

Johnny-Behind is quickly disarmed and taken into custody. Word soon reaches the local authorities that the cow-boys "are preparing to take him out of custody." Fearing their prisoner will either be set free by the cow-boys or lynched by the growing number of angry miners, the officials put the prisoner in a wagon and Constable McKelvey slaps the reins for Tombstone. Halfway there, the miner mob has begun to close in on the wagon. Up ahead, Virgil Earp is out exercising Wyatt's race horse, Dick Nailer. Virgil sees the mob and intercepts McKelvey and his prisoner just as the miners are about to close the gap. The Charleston constable quickly apprises Virgil of the situation and Deuce swings up behind Virgil. Dick Nailer quickly leaves the miner mob in the dust and Virgil pulls up in front of Vogan's saloon where his brother Jim Earp is tending bar.

City Marshal Ben Sippy had been alerted by telegraph of the incoming prisoner and he has secured a score of well-armed men to prevent any rescue or lynching.

Knowing that a justly enraged mob could eventually overpower them, Sippy procures a light wagon and puts the prisoner in, guarded by himself, Wyatt Earp, Virgil Earp, and Deputy Sheriff Behan. As the wagon makes its way through the streets and out of town, a throng of citizens, some armed with rifles and shotguns, advance on the wagon. Sippy halts the wagon and the officers level their weapons on the crowd. The January 27 *Epitaph* will describe the city marshal as being "cool as an iceberg [as] he held the crowd in check." The officers safely remove their prisoner to the safer confines of the Tucson jail.

George Parsons is not so thrilled by the lawmen's work. He notes in his journal: "Many of the miners armed themselves and tried to get at the murderer. Several times, yes a number of times, rushes were made and rifles leveled, causing Mr. Stanley and me to get behind the most available shelter. Terrible excitement, but the officers got through finally and out of town with their man bound for Tucson. This man should have been killed in his tracks. Too much of this kind of business going on. I believe in killing such men as one would a wild animal."

February 1, 1881
Cochise County is created. Tombstone becomes the county seat.

February 5, 1881
Wyatt Earp files water rights in the Huachuca Mountains with three other men: John H. [Doc] Holliday, Rich [Dick] Clark, and James Leavy.

March 15, 1881
The Tombstone stage en route to Benson is attacked by outlaws beyond Drew's Station, killing the driver, Eli Philpot, and a passenger.
Wyatt Earp organizes a posse with John Behan, who has been

JOHNNY BEHAN'S ELECTION DAY POSSE
After a hard day guarding the ballot box against hostile votes, drinking toddies and smoking cigars, Johnny bills the town $1500. (l to r) Peter Spencer, Harry Woods, John Behan, Billy Breakenridge and Frank Stilwell.

HENRY CLAY HOOKER, 1880
Owns the Sierra Bonita Ranch north of Willcox. Known for his "trotters" and western hospitality, Hooker believes guests should "dress" for dinner.

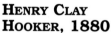

BAT ON THE ROCKS
The Dapper Bat (right) came to Tombstone and stayed only a short time. He was to remain a lifelong friend of Wyatt Earp.

appointed as first sheriff of Cochise County, to pursue the assailants.

Frank King is jailed as one of the outlaws attempting to hold up the stage.

April, 1881

Johnny-Behind-the-Deuce escapes jail in Tucson.

The City of Tombstone, now incorporated, boasts 5,000, making it the second largest community in the territory.

March 20, 1881

The first train makes its way through Arizona establishing connections with Deming, New Mexico, thus opening a new transcontinental route.

June 22, 1881

Tombstone's first disastrous fire breaks out in the Arcade Saloon, east of the Oriental, and one hour later has burned down two square blocks, including 66 stores, saloons, restaurants and business houses. The loss is set at $175,000. The day after the fire, Tombstone starts to rebuild. Two weeks later, most of the saloons are back up, bigger, better and roaring.

June 6, 1881

Chief of Police, Ben Sippy asks for a two-week leave of absence. On motion by the town council, Virgil Earp is appointed to temporarily replace Sippy.

PANTANO POSSE

Wyatt Earp rode in many a posse in his long career, but the one that put in the most miles has to be the Tombstone group of lawmen who rode after Leonard, Crane and Head. Wyatt, Virgil, Johnny Behan and others rode over 300 miles, at one point coming within fifteen miles of Tucson (above) *before riding several horses into the ground.*

WYATT ON DICK NAILER

He came to Tombstone with fifteen thoroughbreds. Wyatt Earp always appreciated good horseflesh. His favorite horse was Dick Nailer (below). This is the same horse Billy Clanton stole and the one Virgil was exercising during the Johnny-Behind-the-Deuce affair. Wyatt always went out on his posses well-armed as you can see.

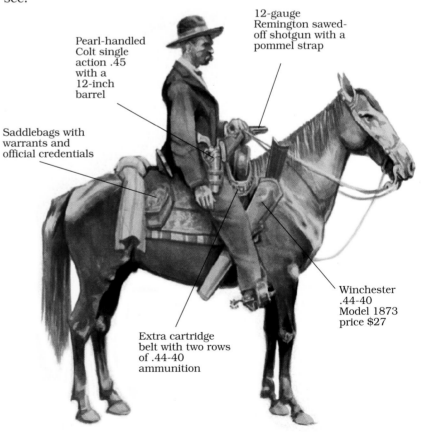

Pearl-handled Colt single action .45 with a 12-inch barrel

12-gauge Remington sawed-off shotgun with a pommel strap

Saddlebags with warrants and official credentials

Winchester .44-40 Model 1873 price $27

Extra cartridge belt with two rows of .44-40 ammunition

Fly's Gallery,   Tombstone, A.T.

GEORGE PARSONS' JOURNAL

He is a bank clerk from San Francisco (left), but when he gets out in the wilds of Arizona, he can't resist going native (below). Parsons diligently kept a journal during his entire stay in Tombstone and his more or less objective views of the events there are an invaluable source. For this reason, he is quoted extensively in this book.

Armed to the Teeth

Wyatt Earp owned over two dozen weapons while he was in Tombstone.

He wasn't alone. Parsons lists in his journal the "numbers on my arms."

- **One Winchester carbine—model 76 .45-60 #11580**

- **One Winchester Rifle—model 73 44-40 #42131**

- **One Smith & Wesson Six-shooter Self Acting .44 calibre #2565**

- **One Smith & Wesson Five-shooter Self Acting .38 calibre #14.066**

- **One Smith & Wesson small .22 calibre-old-#77.554**

- **One Colts single action six-shooter, Frontier .44-40 #72157**

- **One fine hunting knife**

- **Cartridge belts, etc.**

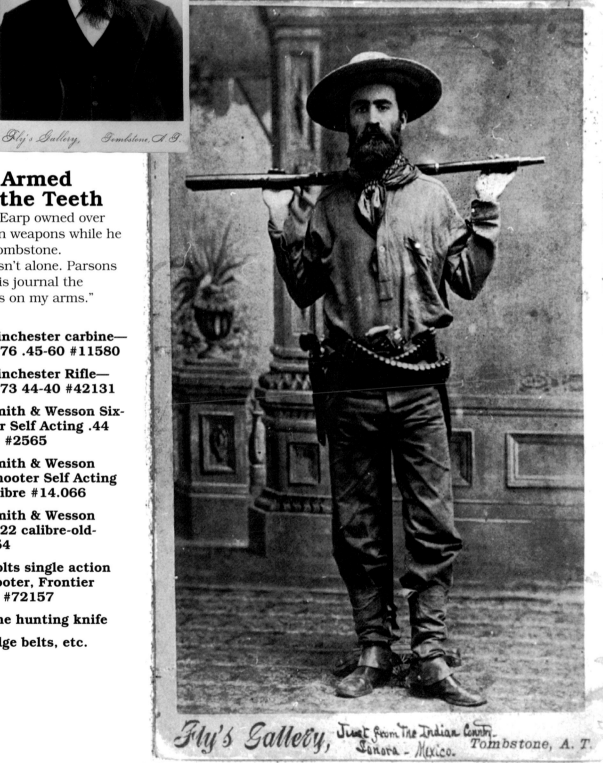

Fly's Gallery, Just from The Indian Country. Sonora - Mexico. Tombstone, A.T.

June 15, 1881

The Earps are not part of Tombstone's upper crust. Allie Earp says that, "we weren't rich minin' folks and important business people, and we lived across the Dead Line." The Earp's residences are at First and Fremont which is in the Mexican area.

As one of the social satellites put it, "The line was pretty well drawn those days. Ordinary women didn't mix with the wives of gamblers and saloon keepers and bartenders, no matter what pretty dresses they had or how nice they were. And the Misses Earp were all good, but they were in that fix and.we just naturally didn't have much to do with them." Allie is hurt by the snubs but at least her husband is moving up.

June 28, 1881

Ben Sippy doesn't return, and with no dissenting votes, Virgil Earp is appointed Chief of Police.

July 2, 1881

President James A. Garfield is shot at the Washington Railroad Station by Charles J. Guiteau, a disgruntled office seeker. Miraculously, Garfield survives the shooting and clings to life for several months. The news is telegraphed across the nation and Tombstone is informed on the same day. In the mining camp, conspiracy theories abound. Parsons believes Garfield was killed because he was going after the railroads. He comments in his journal, "God help this country if the machine has such power as that."

September 8, 1881

The Tombstone-Bisbee stage is held up near Hereford and robbed of twenty-five hundred dollars in the Wells-Fargo box and a mail-sack. Jewelry and seven hundred and fifty dollars in currency are taken from four passengers. There is no shotgun

continued on page 53

A MARRIAGE GONE SOUTH

Celia Ann "Mattie" Blaylock (above) came to Tombstone as Wyatt's wife. If the anecdote on the opposite page is true Wyatt and Mattie had a stormy relationship to say the least, but keep in mind Allie told this story to author Frank Waters after Wyatt became famous and she felt her Virg was getting the short end of the myth-making stick. Allie was obviously close to Mattie and she always resented the woman she felt stole Wyatt away—Josephine "Sadie" Marcus. On balance, it seems Allie is twisting the knife a bit hard here. After all, she blames Wyatt for not taking either one of them uptown—what about her own husband?

CABIN FEVER

The Earp women, Allie, Mattie and Bessie take in sewing jobs to make ends meet. They sew entire canvas tents that are put into immediate service as saloons and stores. After an unusually hard day sewing a striped awning, Allie, in her usual, mischevious way, proposes to Mattie that the two of them go up town and "peek in the big hotels and restaurants where Wyatt never takes us."

A day or two later, while the men are away, Allie and Mattie dress up and walk to town.

They look over the hotels real good and slow down at the Maison Doree and Can Can restaurants (below). They finally stop in front of the Occidental and read the Sunday menu posted in the window (Allie was so impressed, she saved a copy—left)

Allie asks Mattie how'd she like the California Fresh Peach.

At that point, according to Allie, "somebody came up and took us right inside." This "friend" bought the young ladies all different kinds of wines, "fancy good ones in pretty bottles." Many years later, Allie confided that she and Mattie "crossed our hearts never to tell [who it was] and we never did, *even after what happened.*" [Could it have been Johnny Behan?]

The extremely happy girls float home to bed all right and everything would have been jimdandy but Virgil and Wyatt come in unexpectedly for dinner.

Allie remembers Wyatt, mad as a hornet's nest, shouting at Mattie "somethin' dreadful."

"I told you to keep out of town and not to show your face on the streets! I told you!" He keeps shouting.

Sunday Dinner
at the Occidental

SOUPS
Chicken Giblet and Consome, with Egg

FISH
Columbia River Salmon, au Buerre et Noir

RELIEVES
Fillet a bouef, a la Financier
Leg of Lamb, sauce, Oysters

COLD MEATS
Loin of Beef
Loin of Ham
Loin of Pork
Westphalia Ham
Corned Beef
Imported Lunches

BOILED MEATS
Leg of Mutton, Ribs of Beef, Corned Beef and
Cabbage,
Russian River Bacon

ENTREES
Pinionsa Poulett, aux Champignos
Cream Fricassee of Chicken, Asparagus Points
Lapine Domestique, a la Maitre d' Hote
Casserole d' Ritz au Oufs, a la Chinoise
Ducks of Mutton, braze, with Chipoluta Ragout
California Fresh Peach, a la Conde

ROASTS
Loin of Beef
Loin of Mutton
Leg of Pork, Apple Sauce
Sucking Pig, with Jelly
Chicken, and Stuffed Veal

PASTRIES
Peach, Apple, Plum and Custard Pies
English Plum Pudding, Hard Sauce
Lemon Flavor

And we will have it or perish
This dinner is served for 50 cents

EATING OUT IN TOMBSTONE
(above left), *A re-creation of the menu Allie saved from the Occidental Hotel.* (bottom, left) **The Can Can Restaurant,** *1880s. Notice the skylight. The sign at right center says, "No Dogs allowed in Dining Room."*

DEATH ON THE BENSON STAGE

March 15, 1881

The Kinnear and Company stage leaves Tombstone around 7 P.M. with eight passengers and a shipment of bullion worth $80,000. There has been a light fall of snow and the night air is quite cold.

At Contention, the teams are changed and the driver, Bud Philpot changes seats with Bob Paul, the shotgun messenger, so Bud can briefly warm his hands. Just north of Drew's Station, the stage slows down for a grade. It is about ten o'clock.

Several masked men step out of the shadows. One of them shouts "Whoa, boys!"

Bob Paul instinctively drops the reins to grab the shotgun between his legs, as he shouts back, "I hold for no one!"

With that the highwaymen open up, aiming logically at the occupant of the shotgun messenger seat. Bud Philpot is shot through the heart and he pitches forward upon the hooves of his two wheelers. The terrified horses immediately spring into a dead run. Bob Paul risks his life by climbing down onto the dancing wagon tongue as the team and coach careen into the darkness. Against all odds, Paul retrieves the reins which are dragging on the ground. A passenger sitting on the dicky seat at the rear of the coach is shot dead and has toppled off the stage into the road.

Paul gets control of the team and quickly makes his way to Benson, where he telegraphs Tombstone.

March 16, 1881

At daylight a large posse finds seventeen empty rifle-shells in the road where the highwaymen

THE DRIVER'S SEAT TWIST OF FATE

Stage driver Bud Philpot (right) *trades places with the shotgun messenger, Bob Paul, so that Bud can warm his hands for a few minutes, the night air being very cold. When the highwaymen start shooting , they naturally aim for the shotgun messenger.*

had stood. Buckskin Frank Leslie cuts for sign. Anxious for the chase, posse members circle on horseback, quirting their mounts in the brisk morning air. Among them are Bat Masterson (having just arrived from Dodge), John Behan, Billy Breakenridge, the Earp brothers and Marshal Williams.

King For A Day

March 19, 1881

The posse trails the stage robbers to Wheaton's abandoned ranch and finds a badly used up horse. From there the posse heads for Hank Redfield's ranch and Morgan Earp captures one Luther King. He confesses to holding the horse at the Benson stage robbery and names his other accomplices as Bill Leonard, Harry Head and Jim Crane.

Behan puts King under arrest and starts back to Tombstone with the prisoner, accompanied by Billy Breakendridge.

Wyatt and the rest of the posse continue after Leonard, Crane and Head.

They trail for more than three

hundred miles, over the Rincon Mountains, north and west along the Tanque Verde to within fifteen miles of Tucson, then around the Santa Catalinas, through the Oracles and Canada del Oro, east through the Santa Cruz, and back down the San Pedro.

At Benson, the posse wires Tombstone for any particulars. Behan and Breakenridge rejoin the manhunt and the posse at Helm's ranch in the Dragoons.

As the posse takes up the chase again, they are overtaken by Jim Hume, the Chief Special Officer for Wells Fargo. Hume gives the Earps the bitter news that Luther King escaped custody in Tombstone. Evidently, King slipped out the back door of the sheriff's office while one of Behan's deputies was drawing up a bill of sale for the prisoner's horse.

When Wyatt confronts Behan and demands to know why he didn't tell them King had escaped, Behan says he didn't consider it any of Wyatt's business.

How The Epitaph got its name

JOHN CLUM
Editor, Mayor and Postmaster

Although historians still argue as to how Tombstone's fiery newspaper got its name, this version is the funniest:

Ed Schieffelin, the very man who christened the early mines and the town, was riding into the district on a stage with John Clum, who it is said, asked the passengers to suggest a name for the paper he was about to start.

"The Epitaph," said Schieffelin without even taking a breath. "That's the name for a paper that will celebrate in enduring print the deeds and fame of Tombstone."

Clum wasn't convinced. "But epitpahs are usually mere chiselled lies."

"Well," deadpanned Schieffelin, " they tell the truth about as often as newspapers."

JULY 2, 1881

President Garfield is shot two times point-blank at the Washington railroad station. The first bullet struck him in the back and the second barely missed his arm. The President staggered and collapsed, and after a few of the stunned people in the station had regained their wits, he was carried into an office.The 20th president was fluent in Latin and Greek. In fact he could write in Greek with one hand while writing in Latin with the other. Later presidents will write in Greek and talk in Greek all the time.

messenger on the stage, and Levi McDaniels, the driver, offers no resistance when two masked men, one with a shotgun, the other with a pair of Colt's, step into the road with the order to halt and throw down the box. One of the robbers keeps saying "Give up the sugar," and "Don't hide any sugar from us." In spite of the mask, McDaniels recognizes him immediately as Pete Spence. He also recognizes the other road agent as Frank Stilwell. Off in the chaparral McDaniels sees two other men but he cannot identify them.

September 20, 1881

Parsons: "Sad—sad news. Despite the prayers of a Christian world, one of the greatest men the world ever saw...President James A. Garfield died at 10:35 last night at Elbeven Long Branch and a family and nation are plunged in agony. God help the stricken household and be with this country in the present crisis. Away out here on the frontier where politics are quite generally ignored and party lines very loosely drawn, the feeling is more profound than I imagined it would be and as we rode our horses out of town signifying the sad news by the crepe on our saddle pommels, the whole place was being draped in mourning and wore a sad enough aspect as we journey to our mountains home [Parson's mine in the Huachucas] and carried the news to remote places."

October 5, 1881

Mayor Clum, Sheriff Behan, Marshal Virgil Earp, form a posse to track down hostile Indians supposedly in the vicinity of Tombstone.

October 15, 1881

Efforts to force Fremont's resignation as Governor of Arizona had been put on hold because of the shooting of President Garfield in July. And until his death on September 19, the effort was

SAME STREET, DIFFERENT TOWN

We're looking west from Fifth and Allen Streets, the main intersection in Tombstone. What a difference a few months and even days can make in a boomtown. The top photo was taken in 1879 and the bottom one sometime in 1880. The one recognizable building in the top photo is the Golden Eagle Brewery, (see drawing, right).

Less than a year later, the whole street has been reborn including the Golden Eagle Brewery—the two-story building at far right. Virgil Earp was ambushed here as he approached the covered sidewalk where the man is seated. Scattered buckshot peppered the pole in front of the seated man and gouged the wall behind him.

GOLDEN EAGLE BREWERY

ALLEN STREET, 1879

ALLEN STREET, 1880

$50 Reward

The above Reward will be paid to the man who cannot find the

KENO GAME

Which is now running in the

Alhambra Saloon.

FIRST ROLL FREE!

IKE.

THE ORIENTAL SALOON
Wyatt Earp held an interest in this saloon and operated a faro game in the club room. It was in this saloon that the events of October 26 began.

completely shelved. But upon succession of Chester A. Arthur to the presidency they have been renewed. President Arthur announces Fremont's resignation as of October 15, with selection of John J. Gosper as acting-governor pending appointment of a full-fledged successor.

October 17, 1881

Morgan Earp is appointed as a Special Police Officer in Tombstone.

October 23, 1881

Parsons: "Quiet as usual today. Read up my papers and ate my bread and bacon with usual composure. Nothing new yet in these parts. Rather monotonous. I hope this state of things won't continue long."

"Be careful what you

ask for."

—OLD VAQUERO SAYING

NAME CALLING

Tombstonians had a moniker for everyone

Saddler—A bum who lives in the saddle, riding from ranch to ranch and town to town, looking for a handout, a free meal or an easy mark.

Boomer—An opportunist who gravitates to the latest mineral strike. He usually stays until the pickings have peaked, and then heads off for the next boom town. Wyatt Earp was a "Boomer."

Swells—Entrepreneurs looking for sure-thing investments. Wyatt Earp was a "Swell."

Sharpies—Parisites who want to be Swells.

Tyro—A beginner with a gun, as in, "Only a tyro would load all six chambers of his revolver."

Bipeds—Anyone with two feet, which of course includes almost everyone. Indicates a mass of humanity, as in, "Hordes of bipeds descended on the dance."

Mucker—A job in the mines with little esteem. General usage indicates no respect, as in, "Jesse's a bit of a mucker."

Soiled Dove—A prostitute. Also called, Tid Bits, Fallen Frails, Reigning Belles, Doves of the Roost, Cyprians, Demi Monde, Daughters of Sin, Fast Girls, Occupants of Bed Houses.

Imperial Trump—Slang for the Joker in a deck of cards. Used as a mild put-down, as in, "I'm afraid she took him for an Imperial Trump."

Wencher—A woman chaser. Someone who chases after Wenches. Wyatt Earp was a "Wencher."

TOMBSTONE, 1881 LOOKING NORTHWEST

TOMBSTONE SLANG

Blowed up—A lost chance, as in, "We were blowed up and could not find their trail."

Hard sledding—Refers to snow sleds on difficult terrain. Its usage on the frontier refers to having a difficult time convincing someone, as in, " It was hard sledding for Bob Hatch when it came time for his nomination."

Crooking the arm—Getting thrown out of a saloon. Having ones arm "crooked" behind his back and then given the bum's rush, as in, "We were doing fine until they started crooking the arm."

Park—Slang for a prostitute's dwelling, as in, "Let's go take a ride in the park."

Bucking the Tiger—Playing against the faro bank, as in, "We tried to talk Phin into leaving but he was bucking the tiger."

Swag—Having plenty of greenbacks or collateral which allows a gambler to swagger, as in, "The Oriental was full of gentlemen who flashed up considerable swag."

Show case game—A crooked gambling game. Comes from a confidence racket that consisted of setting up a glass show case on the sidewalk to entice unsuspecting pedestrians to buy fake jewelry displayed under glass.

Monkeying with the deadwood—Messing with the discards in a card game.

Play poker—A cautioning phrase, used by a card player who suspects a fellow card player of "monkeying with the deadwood."

*Colt's .45 Buntline Special
with a 16-inch barrel*

*American Model Smith & Wesson .44
with an 8-inch barrel*

*Classic Peacemaker .45
with a 7½-inch barrel*

*Short-barrel Peacemaker .45
with a 4¾-inch barrel*

THE BUNTLINE BATTLE

Did Wyatt Earp carry a Colt with an extra long barrel called the "Buntline Special"?

Researchers working in the 1950s and 60s exposed the Buntline Special as a complete fantasy created by Earp biographer Stuart Lake to give his hero a longer...uh, *weapon* than the other guys. A sort of frontier excalibur. The evidence was convincing—Colt had no records of shipping such a gun to Wyatt. None of Wyatt's friend's ever mentioned such a gun and there is no mention in the frontier press of Earp having carried such a humongous pistol. But wait!

In the Spicer Hearing, A. Bauer testifies, "Wyatt Earp had on a short coat; did not have an overcoat on; it [his pistol] seemed to me an old pistol, pretty large, 14 or 16 inches long, it seemed to me."

Stuart Lake obviously believed a long barreled gun belonging to Wyatt Earp existed because he wrote numerous letters, on file, trying to weasel Wyatt's old friends into giving it to him, "I want it for a keepsake. It is valueless now as a weapon."

Not true, Stuart. A west coast museum allegedly paid $250,000 for a gun on this page they thought was Wyatt's. The Battle of the Buntline is far from over.

ARE YOU JUST HAPPY TO SEE ME?

Long barreled Colt's were in use during this period. This photo, believed to have been taken in Texas in the late 70s, shows a long barrel Colt's with a shoulder stock. Buckskin Frank Leslie ordered a 12-inch custom Colt from Tombstone on January 14, 1881. Perhaps he was inspired by one he saw carried by Wyatt Earp.

Tombstone, after the May 25, 1882 fire.

BUILDING CODES

*Building Codes?
We don't need no steenking building codes!*

August 26, 1880
Parsons: "Very hard rain today. No dry place to flee to. Took refuge in door way for some time as the roof was little protection."

November 5, 1880
Parsons: "Boarding house collapsed today so [we] went to town this afternoon for dinner at Grand [Hotel]."

August 11, 1881
Parsons: "The heavy rains have weakened some adobe walls and this evening the rear end of the recorder's office tumbled into the Grotto cellar. Fortunately, none hurt, but several horses had to be shot from injuries received."

1882
"The outskirts of Tombstone consisted still of huts and tents. A burly miner could be seen stretched upon his cot in a windowless cabin, barely large enough to contain him."
—William Henry Bishop

"Two dangers constantly threaten the world, order and disorder."
—PAUL VALERY

IKE CUTS A DEAL

June 2, 1881
"How'd you like to make $6,000?" Wyatt says to Ike Clanton in front of the Eagle Brewery.

Wyatt wants the glory. He wants to be elected sheriff and if he can get Ike Clanton to give up Leonard, Crane and Head he will get the glory and the office.

Wyatt offers Ike the Wells Fargo reward if he will lead the outlaws to where Wyatt can capture them.

Ike returns on June 6 with Joe Hill and Frank McLaury. Ike wants to know if the offer is "Dead or alive."

Wyatt wires San Francisco on June 7 and shows Ike that, yes, they will pay dead or alive.

Later, Marshall Williams will tip the hand that he knows about Ike's deal with Wyatt. Clanton comes unglued and assumes Wyatt told Doc. If it gets out he is double-crossing the boys, he's dead meat.

Ike confronts Wyatt and accuses him of telling Doc. Earp denies it and sends for Holliday in Tucson to prove it.

Doc denies he knew, but now that Ike has told him, he berates Clanton for being a turncoat.

Ike, who was trying to worm out of a hole, has just dug a bigger one. The next hole he digs will be for his younger brother.

WYATT EARP, 1881

ONE HOT AND BOTHERED LAWMAN

Wyatt and Mattie always come over at noon to eat dinner with Morg and Lou, and Virge and Allie. One hot, summer day Wyatt rushes in followed by the local schoolteacher, Miss Wynn. She had asked Wyatt to sell some raffle tickets in the Oriental and he promised he would to get rid of her. For a week he has been dodging her and here she comes right up to the house.

Wyatt rushes in and hides in the kitchen behind the door and right by the blazin' stove.

Miss Wynn knocks on the door and comes in with the raffle tickets in her hand.

"Did Mr. Wyatt Earp come in here?" she asks, "I saw him comin' down the street."

"No," Allie says, "but he'll be here right soon. Won't you come in?"

Morgan invites her to dinner.

For an hour they keep her at the table, almost stuffing food down her.

Every time Allie goes into the kitchen she can hardly keep from laughing. There's Wyatt in that stuffy hot kitchen, stainin' his shirt, the sweat pourin' off his face.

When Miss Wynn finally leaves, Allie finds out that Wyatt is not amused. He hates being laughed at.

THOSE WHO KNEW WYATT, DESCRIBE HIM

"He was a quiet, but absolutely fearless man; as a peace officer, above reproach. He usually went about in his shirt-sleeves, and with no weapons. He was cool and never excited, but very determined and courageous. He never stirred up trouble, but he never ran away from it or shirked responsibility. He was an ideal peace officer and a fine citizen."
—WILLIAM J. HUNSAKER
　　DEAN OF THE
　　LOS ANGELES BAR, 1931

"Wyatt didn't swear, or call names. He didn't have to raise his voice."
—JACK ARCHER
　　STAGE COACH DRIVER

"Wyatt had courage of a foxy type. He was an efficient officer if he could surround himself with a bunch of killers. He always did that. He never worked alone and turned down several challenges to fight. He was no lone wolf. He was always the leader of a vicious pack...Wyatt was good at tooting his own horn and his veracity could always be questioned."
—PINK SIMMS
　　CHAMPION PISTOL SHOT
　　AND U.S. DEPUTY MARSHAL

"I remember so well his erect carriage and soldierly bearing. He was tall and slender with the most piercing eyes I ever saw."
— MRS. WILDA WEEKS,
　　KINGMAN, ARIZONA

"To Wyatt S. Earp as a slight recognition of his many Christian virtues."
—INSCRIPTION IN A BIBLE
　　GIVEN TO WYATT
　　IN DODGE CITY

Fly's boarding house
where Doc is staying

The O.K. Corral,
rear entrance

The alleyway
where Ike is arrested

Spangenburg's
gun shop

Wyatt's and Virgil's
homes, two blocks
west on Fremont

THIRD STREET

FOURTH STREET

FREMONT STREET

FIFTH STREET

ALLEN STREET

TOUGHNUT STREET

The O.K. Corral,
main entrance

The courtroom
where Ike is fined

Hafford's
Corner

The barbershop
where Behan is
getting his shave

The Grand Hotel

COUNTDOWN TO DESTINY

The Occidental Saloon
where the all night
poker game took place

October 26, 1881

Twenty-seven seconds goes quick. Can it define a
man's life for all time?

As the events of the last several months
intertwine, eight men approach death from
different directions.

Confusing and murky, like random flotsam in a
tide pool, each participant wanders seemingly
without a rudder straight into the black hole of
destiny.

The Oriental Saloon

1880 WAGES

The wages of sin is relative

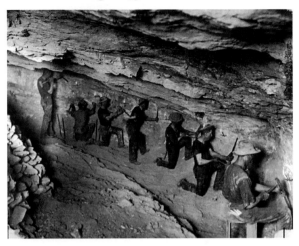

A free-lance hard-rock miner makes $9.50 per foot.

A miner who works above-ground earns $3.50 a day.

A miner who works below-ground earns $4.00 a day.

A soldier's wages is $13 per month.

A carpenter makes $6 a day.

A blacksmith makes $6 a day.

A mason makes $6 a day.

A engineer makes $6 a day.

A laborer makes $3 a day.

A cook earns between $50 to $75 per month.

A faro dealer makes $6 per four hour shift.

A cow-boy makes $30 a month.

A" soiled dove" charges twenty-five cents to $1 a throw.
She takes home half.

A shotgun messenger earns $125 a month.

MADAME MOUSTACHE

BLOND MARY

DUTCH ANNIE

Competition between the Tombstone Madams was stiff.

October 25, 1881

Ike Clanton, his younger brother Billy, Tom and Frank McLaury, ride into Jack Chandler's milk ranch at the foot of the Dragoon mountains, for breakfast. Around the breakfast table, the McLaury's and Clantons make a plan to meet the following day, in the early afternoon at the Grand Hotel in Tombstone. After breakfast, Ike Clanton and Tom McLaury hitch up a spring wagon loaded with beef and rack out on the road with a saddle horse tied on behind the rig. The ten mile trip is mostly downhill and they arrive in Tombstone between 10 and 11 o'clock in the morning and stable their horses and park their wagon in the West End Corral.

Meanwhile, back out at Chandler's milk ranch, Billy Clanton and Frank McLaury mount up and make one more horseback sweep through the Antelope Springs area looking for strays they might have missed. They will take their time and spend the night out in the chaparral, before turning and making the thirteen mile ride into Tombstone.

**Early Evening
October 25, 1881**

Ike and Tom take in the town. They have been out on the range for weeks and its time to knock the moss off their antlers. Clanton and McLaury start with drinks at the Grand, which is the cow-boy's designated hangout. They talk with old friends and catch up on the latest border wars. Later, they make the rounds trying not to miss any of the 66 saloons that saturate the city limits. Ike bucks the Tiger, Tom takes in a little mexican monte and looks for a good game of poker.

Around eleven, Tom goes his own way, while Ike continues to take in the town. About 1 A.M. Ike goes into the Alhambra for a bite. While he's eating, Doc Holliday comes in and starts to abuse him and call him every name in the

*Three Slaughter cow-boys, 1881
Billy Quinn, seated. The other two are unidentified.*

Fly's Gallery, Tombstone, A. T.

"The leading cattle-men had a Southern cut and accent, and hailed originally from Missouri or Texas. Some appeared in full black broadcloth, accompanied by the usual wide sombrero. The landlord of our hotel described them as "perfect gentlemen," some of them good at the bar for as high as $20 or $25 a day."
—WILLIAM HENRY BISHOP, 1882

SEEING TRIPLE

Wyatt recalled to Stuart Lake in 1928 how confused Tombstonians became at the incredible physical likeness between the three brothers–Wyatt, Virgil and Morgan. When the first council of Tombstone wished to appoint Virgil Earp as town marshal, the appointed messenger walked up and handed the badge to Wyatt. On another occasion, E.B. Gage gave a saddle horse to Morgan in the belief that he was transferring ownership to Wyatt, who had sought to purchase the animal earlier.

Finally, the sporting crowd placed bets and to settle the argument, the three Earps were weighed and measured. According to Wyatt, "Boots off, there wasn't three pounds difference in our weights, and not one of us scaled above a hundred and fifty-eight. Virg was the heaviest, Morg a shade heavier than I. When you add that each of us had wavy, light-brown hair, blue eyes, and a mustache of the sweeping variety then in Western fashion, you may understand why our comings and goings often were reported inaccurately and why certain persons in Arizona ascribed supernatural qualities to the Earps."

"Together they looked alike as three peas in a pod—the same height, size and mustaches. In Tombstone later men were always mistakin' one for another."
—ALLIE EARP

book. Ike tries to calm Holliday down, but Doc is drunk and tries to bully Ike into fighting. Ike sees Morgan and Wyatt just beyond with their hands on their pistols and he knows they are all trying to set him up.

As Ike leaves he asks Wyatt not to shoot him in the back.

Wyatt's version of the same event is somewhat different.

In the early evening, Doc Holliday confronts Ike Clanton in the Alhambra lunch room. Holliday rakes Clanton over the coals about his accusations. Ike denies that he has made any and Doc calls him a "damned liar." The two quarrel for three or four minutes, both of them getting louder and more threatening. Wyatt is eating lunch at the counter and calls his brother Morgan in to break them up. Acting in his official capacity as an officer, Morgan jumps the lunch room counter from the Alhambra bar and goes into the lunch room and takes Holliday by the arm and leads him into the street. Unfortunately, Ike Clanton follows them out and the verbal abuse begins again.

Coming out of the Occidental, City Marshal Virgil Earp quickly comes between the two and threatens to arrest them both if they don't stop. Both men realize Virgil is not bluffing—having previously arrested his own boss, Mayor Clum for speeding in a buggy, and his own brother, Wyatt, for fighting.

Doc slithers off, Ike retires to the Grand Hotel, Morgan heads for home and Virgil goes back into the Occidental saloon. Wyatt goes across to the Eagle Brewery where he has a faro game going that has not closed. Wyatt hangs around for a few moments and then steps outside. He is somewhat surprised to come face to face with Ike Clanton, who asks Wyatt if he will go for a walk. Wyatt tells Ike he can't go far on account of the faro game, so they walk about half the length of the Brewery building, up

TOMBSTONE COW-BOY, 1885
W. Upward cuts a classic cow-boy pose. This is a very good example of the "stockmen style" around Cochise County in the 80s—highback saddle, high-heeled boots, shotgun chaps,Mexican loop holster with .45, vest, dark shirt and wide, flat-brimmed hat. Perfect.

DEPUTY BILLY BREAKENRIDGE

Fifth Street. Drunk, and full of confidence when no one is around, Ike tells Wyatt that in the morning he will have "man for man."

Wyatt tells Clanton he doesn't want to fight "because there is no money in it." Ike continues his harangue—It's time to fetch this feud to a close. Fed up with the whiskey talk, Wyatt finally says, "Go home Ike, you talk too much for a fighting man."

With that Wyatt leaves Ike Clanton with his hot air and goes back into the Eagle Brewery to collect his faro money and put it in the safe. On his way down Allen Street, Wyatt meets Doc and they walk together down Allen and then up Fourth to Fremont and then west to Fly's where Doc is rooming. As Wyatt continues on towards his house at First Street and Fremont, neither of them could possibly realize that they will make this same walk again very soon, but under quite different circumstances.

PART TWO

The Gunfight

THE GUNFIGHT- EARPS VERSION

6:15 A.M.

Virgil Earp is leaving the all-night poker game in the Occidental when Ike Clanton stops him and asks him to carry a message to Doc Holliday. Ike's message is: "The damned son of a bitch has got to fight."

When Virgil informs Ike that he cannot carry that message because he is an officer of the law, Ike turns on the Marshal and spits, "You may have to fight before you know it."

Virgil makes no reply and goes home to bed.

8:45 A.M.

Ned Boyle wakes Wyatt Earp at his home on Fremont and tells him of Ike's threats. Boyle quotes Clanton as saying, "As soon as those damned Earps make their appearance on the street today, the ball will open. We are here to make a fight. We are looking for the sons of bitches." Wyatt stays in bed awhile and then rises and goes down to the Oriental saloon. Harry Jones tells Wyatt that Ike is armed with a Winchester and a six-shooter and "hunting you boys."

9:00 A.M.

Ike Clanton goes into Kelly's Wine House. He will continue drinking and making threats there until eleven when he leaves and goes into Hafford's.

Officer Andy Bronk comes down to Virgil's house for a commitment regarding a prisoner. While Virgil is getting it, Bronk says, "You had better get up. There is liable to be hell. Ike Clanton has threatened to kill Holliday as soon as he gets up. He's counting you fellows in too." Virgil waves Bronk off and goes back to bed, hoping the situation will burn off by itself.

IKE CLANTON

READ'EM AND WEEP
Tom McLaury (above left) *shows low to* (l to r) *Virgil Earp, an unidentified man, John Behan and Ike Clanton. This all-night card game in the Occidental, pairing these players, proves conclusively that life is stranger than any fiction. By daylight, Ike* (left) *is completely snockered. He will continue drinking right up to the time when the ball opens.*

"Fight is my racket. All I want is four feet of ground."
—IKE CLANTON

*"Dark and high the war clouds were piling.
Forked hatreds snaked flamingly
across the blind gloom, and vengeance
threatened in rumbling thunder growls.
The red deluge was about to burst.
Nothing now could hold back the storm."*
—WALTER NOBLE BURNS

9:20 A.M.

Virgil Earp is awakened again and told that Ike is hunting him with a Winchester and yelling at passerbys that "As soon as the Earps show, the ball will open!"

12:10 P.M.

Ike is in Hafford's complaining that the Earps have not shown. He leaves in a huff to go hunt Holliday.

Kate Holliday rises from her bed in Fly's boarding house and goes into the photo gallery. A man comes in with a rifle, looks around and leaves. Moments later, Mrs. Fly comes into where Kate is and says, "Ike Clanton is looking for Doc." Mrs. Holliday immediately wakes Doc and informs him that Ike Clanton is hunting him with a rifle. Doc sits up in bed and replies, "If God will let me live long enough, he will see me."

12:15 P.M.

Wyatt leaves the Oriental, and runs into Virgil. They compare notes and split up, Wyatt taking Allen street and Virgil going up Fifth Street and turning west on Fremont.

12:20 P.M.

"Hello Ike, any new war?" is John Clum's ironic greeting as he passes Ike talking under his breath to someone on the corner of Fourth and Fremont in front of the Post Office. Mayor Clum is on his way to lunch at the Grand Hotel and has just left his office at the Epitaph. The mayor has no idea of the impending storm and walks on oblivious.

12:30 P.M.

Virgil finds Ike Clanton on Fourth Street between Fremont and Allen in the mouth of an alleyway, with a Winchester rifle in his hand and a six-shooter stuck down his breeches. Virgil walks up behind him and grabs the rifle in his left hand. Taken by surprise, Ike half turns and then lets go of the Winchester and

FRANK MCLAURY
The most dangerous member of the cow-boy group was Frank McLaury. And as we shall see — the best shot. Evidently Frank shaved the Imperial (chin whiskers) before the fight.

starts to draw his six-shooter. Virgil hits him over the head with his pistol. Ike falls to his knees and is disarmed. Virgil asks Clanton if he was hunting for him and Ike tells Earp yes, and adds, "If I had seen you a second sooner I would have killed you."

12:35 P.M.

Virgil escorts Ike to Judge Wallace's courtroom, but the magistrate is not there. Ike is left in charge of policeman Morgan Earp, while Virgil goes to get the judge. Virgil wants to get this over quickly and back to bed.

12:40 P.M.

Wyatt Earp comes in and sits down on a bench opposite Ike. Clanton looks over at Wyatt and says, "I will get even with all of you for this. If I had a six-shooter now I would make a fight with all of you." Morgan, who is standing to the right of Wyatt, holding the confiscated weapons, says to Ike, "If you want to make a fight right bad, I will give you this one," and holds out Clanton's own six-shooter. Ike starts to get up and take it when Campbell, the deputy sheriff, pushes Clanton back in his seat, telling Ike that he will not allow any fuss.

Wyatt then says to Ike, "You damned dirty cow thief. You have been threatening our lives and I know it. I think I would be justified in shooting you down any place I should meet you. But if you are anxious to make a fight, I will go anywhere on earth to make a fight with you—even over to the Sam Simon, among your own crowd."

Clanton replies, "I will see you after I get through here. I only want four feet of ground to fight on."

12:55 P.M.

After Wallace's examination of Clanton (Ike is fined $27.50), Virgil asks him where he wants his arms left and Ike says,

THE GUNFIGHT AT THE O.K. CORRAL

Of course it never happened in the corral, but it sure sounds good. These two views of the O.K. Corral are the only known photographs of the famous stable and were taken about 1890.(The caption on the back says the buggy belongs to Dr. George Willis who ironically was shot to death in the corral in 1890 by a disgruntled business associate.) It was through this corral that the cow-boys walked on their way to Fremont Street and the fight.

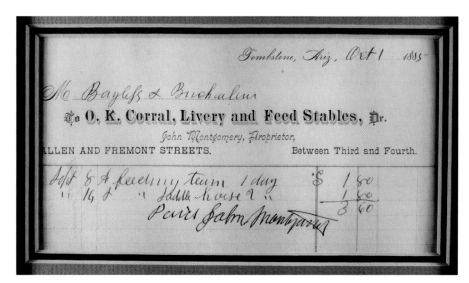

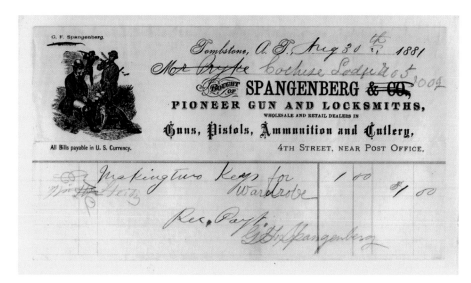

"There appeared to be something of a standing feud between the miners and the cow-boys, and there was besides a faction of "town cow-boys" organized against the "country cow-boys."
—WILLIAM HENRY BISHOP, 1882

"Anywhere I can get them, for you hit me over the head with your six-shooter." Virgil takes Ike's weapons to the Grand Hotel bar and leaves them.

12:57 P.M.

Wyatt Earp steps out of the courtroom and meets Tom McLaury, who says to Earp, "If you want to make a fight, I will make a fight with you, anywhere." Wyatt says, "All right, make a fight here," and at the same time slaps McLaury in the face with his left hand, while drawing his pistol with his right. McLaury has a pistol in plain sight on his right hip, in his pants, but makes no move to draw it. Wyatt tells him, "Jerk your gun and use it." Tom makes no reply and Wyatt hits him on the head with his six-shooter and walks away.

1:10 P.M.

Wyatt walks down to Hafford's corner, goes inside the saloon and buys a cigar. He then steps outside and stands by the door. In a few moments, Frank McLaury and William Clanton walk by in a warlike mood. They are coming from the Grand Hotel and turn up Fourth, going into Spangenberg's gunsmith shop where they meet Tom McLaury and Ike. Wyatt boldly follows them up to see what they are going to do.

1:17 P.M.

A dozen onlookers are gathered in front of Spangenberg's Gunsmith Shop. A horse has joined them up on the sidewalk with his head in the door of the gunshop. Wyatt, as deputy city marshal, spots the horse illegally parked and walks up to pull the horse off the sidewalk. Reaching in the door, Wyatt grabs the horse's bit and commences to back him off the sidewalk. As he does so, Frank McLaury rushes outside and takes the reins from Earp and backs his horse into the street. Virgil, hearing that his brother is facing the cow-boys alone, quickly comes down to assist Wyatt and they both witness the cow-boys inside putting cartridges in their gunbelts.

1:18 P.M.

Virgil is approached by several miners who tell him that two more cow-boys just rode in. Ike was seen walking up to them and telling them about being hit over the head with a six-shooter. One of the men on horseback was overheard to say, "Now is our time to make a fight." A rumor quickly spreads that Ike has telegraphed Charleston for more cow-boys to join him.

Virgil Earp walks down to the Wells Fargo Express office and fetches his shotgun.

1:37 P.M.

The cow-boys have re-armed themselves and they come out of the gun shop and walk back down Fourth to where the Earps are gathered on Hafford's corner. Both sides eye each other warily as the cow-boys turn west on Allen and disappear into the Dunbar Corral.

1:52 P.M.

Representatives of the Citizen's Safety Committee approach Virgil Earp, offering their help in disarming the cow-boys. Virgil tells his brother Wyatt to keep the peace while he's gone and to move the crowd off the sidewalk around Hafford's corner. Virgil steps off forty feet to talk with the Safety Committee.

2:10 P.M.

The cow-boys leave the Dunbar Corral and go into the O.K. Corral. A train engineer, who is just new in town overhears the cow-boys' threats against the Earps, as he passes them. The engineer, who knows none of the principals, inquires to the assembled throng

"There was a tall man with gray clothes and broad hat standing about the middle of the street..."
—C.H. LIGHT
describing Doc Holliday standing on Allen Street

"Doc Holliday met Billy Clanton about 20 minutes before and shook hands with him and told him he was pleased to meet him."
—IKE CLANTON

HAFFORD'S CORNER
Morgan and Doc stand in the middle of Allen Street and look for signs of the cow-boys. The crowd in front of Hafford's grew quite large and definitely became a factor in egging on the Earps.

(l to r) **VIRGIL EARP, J. L. FONCK AND WYATT EARP**

"I saw the Marshal in the doorway of a vacant store with a double-barreled shotgun. He had the shot-gun in his left hand."
—P.H. Fellehy

(l to r) *Wyatt Earp, Morgan Earp, Virgil Earp and Doc Holliday start out on their little stroll.*

at Hafford's as to where he can find Earp. He informs Virgil that all the cow-boys are armed, spitting threats and preparing for a fight as they move through the corral.

2:17 P.M.

The crowd at Hafford's corner is getting larger. Doc and Morgan stand in the middle of the intersection and look for signs of the cow-boys. Moments later they see Frank McLaury standing on the southwest corner of Fourth and Fremont. He has evidently walked through the corral and come out onto Fremont Street. Both parties look for signs of movement and Frank stays partially hidden as he surveys the Earp's position.

John Behan

2:18 P.M.

Virgil takes a drink with Sheriff Johnny Behan in Hafford's saloon. Virgil asks Behan to accompany him and go help "disarm these parties." Johnny refuses, saying that there would sure be a fight if Earp goes down there. Instead, Behan offers to go down alone and see if he can disarm them. While they are talking at the bar, two separate men come up to Virgil and offer assistance and arms. One of them, W. B. Murray, takes Virgil off to one side and says, "I have been looking into this matter and know you are going to have trouble. I can get twenty-five armed men at a moment's notice. If you want them, say so." Virgil tells him that as long as the cow-boys stay in the O.K. Corral, he will not go down to disarm them because it is not illegal to carry firearms in a livery stable. "However," Virgil clarifies for Murray, "if they come out on the street, I will take their arms off and arrest them."

As Virgil rejoins Behan at the bar, the Sheriff says, "What does that son of a bitch of a strangler (a reference to vigilante hanging) want?"

2:28 P.M.

Behan leaves Hafford's to go talk with the cow-boys. He finds Frank McLaury standing at Fourth and Fremont. He tells Frank to come with him and they walk down to where the others are standing—west of the O.K. Corral rear entrance, just beyond Fly's in the side yard, just outside the window where Doc is boarding.

2:34 P.M.

W.A. Cuddy, a bartender and theatrical manager, hears about the impending "fuss" in the post office. Curious, he walks down as far as Fly's house and sees Sheriff Behan talking to "four farmers." As Cuddy walks up close, "one of them, Mr. William Clanton, put his hand on his pistol, as if in fear of somebody—when he recognized me, he removed his hand."

2:42 P.M.

Virgil rejoins his brothers and the crowd on the corner. John L. Fonk comes up to him and warns him of the cow-boy's threats. "Shortly after he [Behan] left," Virgil says, "I was notified that [the cow-boys] were on Fremont Street, and I called on Wyatt and Morgan Earp and Doc Holliday to go help me disarm the Clantons and McLaurys." Virgil hands the Wells Fargo shotgun to Doc and takes Holliday's cane. He instructs the dentist to keep the weapon under his coat. so as not to create any excitement going down the street. After the exchange Virgil says, "Come along," and the four blonds set out to find and disarm the cow-boys.

2:46 P.M.

From Hafford's corner, the four start up Fourth Street. At this point the Earps and Holliday do not know exactly where and how

As the Earps and Holliday begin their infamous walk it is safe to say none of them had any idea they were stepping into history.

many cow-boys there will be. More may have ridden in and joined their compadres from the west end of town, without the lawmen knowing it. Morg worries out loud that they may be on horseback. Wyatt dismisses his fear by calmly stating that they will just shoot the horses and capture them. As

the four clear the corner and turn onto Fremont, they still cannot see their quarry. All four squint and scan the street from top to bottom, across and backwards. Tufts of cold wind sting their cheeks and tug at their coats, exposing the shotgun tucked under Holliday's coat. They keep walking. Still no sign of the cow-boys. Is it a trap? Finally, as Virgil gets about to Union Market (formerly Bauer's), he sees six men standing in a vacant lot just west of Fly's. The parties are Ike and Billy Clanton, Tom and Frank McLaury, Johnny Behan and Billy the Kid Claiborne.

THE ROUTE TAKEN BY THE EARPS

The four men walked in a tight knot up Fourth Street and then turned west into the middle of Fremont. Once they spotted the cow-boys, Virgil steered his men back onto the sidewalk.

Tom and Frank McLaury anticipate the motive of the oncoming Earps.

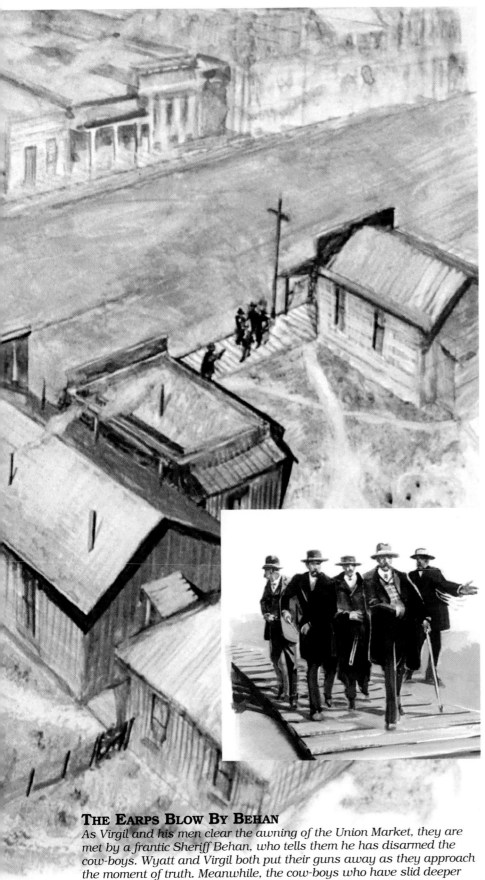

THE EARPS BLOW BY BEHAN

As Virgil and his men clear the awning of the Union Market, they are met by a frantic Sheriff Behan, who tells them he has disarmed the cow-boys. Wyatt and Virgil both put their guns away as they approach the moment of truth. Meanwhile, the cow-boys who have slid deeper into the lot, can't see the Earps, (the fences in the vacant lot are speculative, based on the overwhelming evidence that all the cow-boys tried to leave the lot by way of the street.) The next 27 seconds will define Wyatt Earp's life for the ages.

As they clear the Union Butcher Shop awning, the Earps see Johnny Behan leave the cow-boys and come towards them at a quick walk. Every few steps he looks back over his shoulder as though he expects danger of some kind. Behan throws both hands up in an attempt to physically corral the oncoming Earps. They ignore him and walk on. Waving his arms, Johnny exclaims to Virgil, "For God's sake, don't go down there or they will murder you!" Virgil is resolute and he continues walking as he answers, "Johnny, I am going down to disarm them." As the Earps pass Behan, they hear the Sheriff say, "I have disarmed them all." With that remark, Virgil moves the pistol in his waistband clear around to his left hip and changes the walking stick to his right hand. Wyatt sticks his pistol in his overcoat pocket.

2:47 P.M.

Sensing the impending moment of truth, the cow-boys have slid deeper into the vacant lot to where the Earps can't see them. All Virgil now sees is "about half a horse." As Virgil clears the corner of Fly's, the cow-boys come into view, all in a row, with Ike standing slightly in front. Billy Clanton and Frank McLaury have their hands on their six-shooters. Tom McLaury has his hand on a Winchester rifle on a horse. Virgil, the ranking lawman, immediately takes command of the situation and says, "Boys, throw up your hands. I want your guns." There is a "click-click" sound as Billy and Frank cock their guns. Ike makes a move for his breast pocket. Alarmed, it is Virgil's turn to raise

Billy Clanton (left) *slams against the house, while Virgil* (right) *fires at him. Behind Virgil, Morgan has been hit and is down while Wyatt shoots at the withers of Tom McLaury's horse. Frank McLaury is just about to fire—he will hit Virgil in the calf.*

both hands up, and he says, "Hold on, I don't want that!"

As he says this, Billy Clanton throws his six-shooter down at full-cock.

2:47:02 P.M.

Wyatt pulls his pistol from his overcoat pocket. Later, he will testifiy that "Billy Clanton leveled his pistol at me, but I did not aim at him, I knew Frank McLaury had the reputation of being a good shot and a dangerous man, and I aimed at Frank McLaury. The first two shots were fired by Billy Clanton and myself, he shooting at me, and I shooting at Frank McLaury. I don't know which was fired first. We fired almost together." Wyatt's shot hits Frank square in the belly, the young Clanton misses. Wyatt testifies later that "The fight then became general."

2:47:04 P.M.

With the firing of the first two shots, Tom McLaury's horse comes unglued and Tom cannot retrieve his Winchester. Using the animal as a breastwork, he pulls a pistol from underneath his long

blue blouse and fires twice over the horse's back.

2:47:05 P.M.

Virgil changes the cane to his left hand and goes to shooting. He fires once at Frank McLaury and three at Billy Clanton. Still holding the reins of his horse, Frank McLaury staggers towards the street, firing as he goes. For a long moment, Tom McLaury and his spinning horse block the cow-boys in the lot and keep them directly in harm's way.

2:47:09 P.M.

After the first four shots, Ike Clanton runs up and grabs Wyatt's left arm. Wyatt can see that he has no weapon in his hand and says, "This fight has commenced. Go to fighting, or get away." With that, Wyatt pushes him away with his left hand and Clanton, without stopping, runs into the front of the lodging house, out through the back door, onto the back landing, by Behan, over Billy Claiborne, into the photography gallery, through the hall, out the back, around the gallery corner, over the fence,

Tight Quarters

The open space between Fly's and the house west of there, was only 18 feet. The combatants could literally reach out and touch each other at the outset. Billy Clanton (above) *emptied his pistol and hit no one.*

*"You sons of bitches
have been looking
for a fight
and now you
can have it."*
—WYATT EARP

ONE COOL CUSTOMER

The Epitaph *reported that
Wyatt Earp stood and fired
"as cool as a cucumber."
That and the fact that he was
the only principal in the fight
who escaped unscratched (Ike
doesn't count—he left after
the first four shots.) The myth
machinery was starting to
grind. Wyatt was a very
lucky man—when it
came to bullets.*

between the outhouses, across
Allen, under the freight wagon,
into Kellog's saloon, past the faro
tables, through the fiddler, out the
back door, down the alley and into
Alfred Henry Emanuel's building
on Toughnut Street, where he
secures himself behind a barrel of
mescal.

2:47:15 P.M.

In the midst of the loud
explosions, the agonized screams
and the billowing black powder,
the cow-boy horses have "gone
south" and sunfish down the
street. Frank McLaury tries to
retreat across the street, running
past Holliday. (Wyatt later
wondered if Frank was seeking
refuge in the house of a woman he
was seeing who lived across the
street.) He stops near an adobe
building opposite the lot, turns
and teeters with his pistol across
his arm, the pistol in his right
hand and resting on his left arm.
He aims at Doc and says, "I've got
you now."

2:47:19 P.M.

Holliday, with his emaciated
frame, turns sideways towards
McLaury, aims back and says,
"You're a daisy if you do."

Morgan Earp, rises to a sitting
position and fires at Frank
McLaury. The ball takes effect
below the right ear killing him
instantly.

Frank had been deadly
accurate with his pistol. He hit
Morgan across the shoulders,
Virgil in the right calf, Doc on the
hip and he punctured Wyatt's
coat, missing him by an inch. Had
Frank not been shot on the first
exchange, he may have
singlehandedly killed them all .

2:47:25 P.M.

Virgil Earp directs Wyatt and
Morgan to back out of the lot into
Fremont Street. Doc Holliday
remains on Fremont Street for the
entire fight, finally moving north
to accost a dying Frank McLaury.
"The son of a bitch has shot me,

and I mean to kill him!" Doc screams as he tries to make his way through the crowd that has quickly gathered after the fight.

2:47:27 P.M.

The firing stops. There have been over thirty shots fired in less than thirty seconds. The fusillade came in awkward bursts—lead spasms—starting, stopping, and then multiple shots seemingly on top of each other. The sound of grunts and screams and metal on bone, the harrowing "click-click" of seven triggers has died away, leaving only the moaning of the dying. Camilius S. Fly runs out from his boarding house and takes the pistol from Billy Clanton's hand. As he gasps for air, the dying Clanton gamely asks for more cartridges.

The Vizina Mine whistle blows, signaling the Vigilance Committee to assemble for an emergency. Within minutes they are mobilized by twos in the center of Fremont Street.

As seventy armed men converge on the scene, the Earps and Holliday have an anxious moment as they realize that they are out of bullets and wonder if the approaching throng is friend or foe.

John Behan and many others step out from hiding and wade through the heavy smoke. The Sheriff tries to take control of the situation and says to Wyatt, "I want to see you." Earp replies, "I won't be arrested now. You threw us, Johnny."

2:49 P.M.

The wounded Earps are taken to a "drug store" uptown where their wounds are dressed. From there, Virgil and Morgan are loaded in the town hack and pulled by hand to their home. Billy Clanton lingers for half an hour thrashing around and yelling. Later, Billy, Tom and Frank McLaury are taken to the Dexter Corral and placed in a back room to await the undertaker.

"One man who had lately arrived from the East had a ball pass through his pants. He left for home this morning."
—THE NUGGET

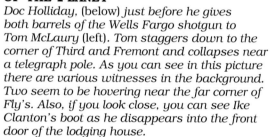

TOM MCLAURY'S LAST VIEW OF THE PLANET

Doc Holliday, (below) just before he gives both barrels of the Wells Fargo shotgun to Tom McLaury (left). Tom staggers down to the corner of Third and Fremont and collapses near a telegraph pole. As you can see in this picture there are various witnesses in the background. Two seem to be hovering near the far corner of Fly's. Also, if you look close, you can see Ike Clanton's boot as he disappears into the front door of the lodging house.

"That Wyatt Earp did wilfully, unlawfully, deliberately, premeditatedly, feloniously, and with malice aforethought, kill or murder William Clanton, Thomas McLaury, and Frank McLaury."
—A WARRANT ISSUED BEFORE JUSTICE OF THE PEACE J. B. SMITH

THE COW-BOY VERSION

Five shots were fired by the Earp party before any of the cow-boys attempted to fight back. Only two, Billy Clanton and Frank McLaury, even had a weapon, and both of theirs were holstered. As the Marshal ordered them to raise their hands, the Clantons and McLaurys complied completely, only to be shot down like dogs.

the agricultural situation of Arizona, and
will visit New Mexico on his way east.

The Funeral.

The funeral of the McLowry brothers
and Clanton yesterday was numerically,
one of the largest ever witnessed in Tombstone. It took place at 3:30 from the
undertaking rooms of Messrs. Ritter &
Ream. The procession, headed by the
Tombstone brass band, moved down Allen
street, and thence to the cemetery. The
sidewalks were densely packed for three
or four blocks. The body of Clanton was
in the first hearse, and those of the two
brothers in the second, side by side, and
were interred in the same grave. It was a
most impressive and saddening sight, and
such a one as it is to be hoped may never
occur again in this community.

Passenger Departures.

BY SANDY BOB'S STAGE.

Dr. Evarts, J Stevenson, J Martin, H
O'Niel, H Mallard and one Mexican.

BY KINNEAR'S LINE.

H Cox, T E Hicks.

Justice's Court.

REMAINS OF MᶜLAURY-EARP
TOMBSTONE ARIZONA

MURDERED ON THE STREETS OF TOMBSTONE

Or so said the sign Ike placed so everyone could see it. (l to r) Tom McLaury, Frank McLaury and Billy Clanton. Evidently Frank shaved his imperial (chin whiskers) sometime before the fight.

"At the morgue the bodies of the three slain cow-boys lay side by side, covered with a sheet. Very little blood appeared on their clothing, and only on the face of young Billy Clanton was there any distortion of the features or evidence of pain in dying. The features of the two McLaury boys look as calm and placid in death as if they had died peaceably."
—The Nugget

October 29, 1881

Pending investigation of charges, Mayor Clum moves that Virgil Earp be temporarily suspended and James Flynn act as Chief of Police during the suspension. Virgil has served a total of 163 days.

Ike Clanton files murder charges against the Earps and Holliday with Justice Wells Spicer.

October 31, 1881

Justice Wells Spicer begins a hearing to determine if the Earps and Holliday should be bound over for a full-scale murder hearing in District Court.

Just prior to this, the Virgil Earp residence receives a nighttime visit from a "veiled visitor" whom they later ascertain was a man dressed as a woman. When Jim Earp answered the door, the visitor mumbled something about wrong house and he/she quickly left. The Earps, fearing the visitor was an assassin, move into the Cosmopolitan Hotel.

Parsons writes in his journal: "Met Wyatt Earp in hotel who took me in to see Virgil this evening, He's getting along well. Morgan too. Looks bad for them all thus far."

November 2, 1881

Parsons buys some Mexican jewelry for Christmas presents to send back east. He says he "got them cheap only $16.75 broach for sister and hair ornaments for Nathalie and Strallus. All of equal value and quite choice and rare. Sent care of sister by Xpress."

November 4, 1881

Will R. McLaury arrives in Tombstone from his home in Fort Worth, Texas. He is the brother of the dead cow-boys and an attorney. He immediately joins the prosecution team and succeeds in getting Wyatt and Doc remanded to jail without bail (Virgil and

Morgan are exempted because of their wounds.)

The two accused murderers are arrested by H.M. Woods on November 7 and held in the makeshift jail on Sixth Street. For sixteen days, heavily armed friends take turns guarding the two-room clap-board hoosegow around the clock to avoid an assassination attempt by the cow-boys.

Later that same night, Parsons writes that he "went to a stag meeting a while but fled at approach of ladies not being in proper costume."

November 11, 1881

"Cold again last night and a little more snow. Guess we had half inch of snow and an inch or more of ice," Parsons records.

November 12, 1881

Parsons: "Have resumed my bathing in creek. The fellows here think I've got a terrible gall to sit down and wash in the cold mountain stream."

November 29, 1881

The taking of testimony is completed in the Wells Spicer hearing and his decision is published in the Nugget two days later. The Earps and Holliday are completely exonerated.

December 10, 1881

Tombstone is tense. Parsons writes in his journal that "Doc snuffed the light with revolver tonight in his office and about 500 people were on hand in a minute. Great excitement. Done for devilment."

December 14, 1881

The Tombstone stage heading for Benson with Mayor Clum aboard is attacked by unknown assailants and Clum escapes into the darkness to save his life.

December 16, 1881

An editorial in the *Epitaph*

states: "Since the late unfortunate affair [the gunfight], rumors have been rife of the intended assassination of not only the Earp brothers, but of Marshal Williams, Mayor Clum, Judge Spicer and Thomas Fitch. Why the feeling of deadly hatred should exist in relation to the Earps and Holliday, every one can understand; but as against the others, it is one of those inscrutable mysteries that none but the most depraved can possibly assign a reason for."

December, 1881

President Arthur warns the citizens of Cochise County to clean up the lawlessness or he will impose martial law.

December 17, 1881

Judge Wells Spicer receives an anonymous letter warning him that it is "only a matter of time," before he is not among the living. "Sooner or later" the missive states, he will get his just desserts. Doc Holliday receives a neat little box wrapped in tissue paper and tied with a pink ribbon. Bundled up in soft white cotton is a forty-five calibre bullet. A little card is signed "Well Wisher" and says, "I've got another one just like this that I'm going to give you some day—in the neck."

December 21, 1881

The Bird Cage Variety Theatre opens in Tombstone. It is owned and operated by William and Lotty Hutchinson who book their talent from San Francisco. The place is an immediate success and it's a great resort for both factions and the bar does a rushing business.

December 28, 1881

It is a Wednesday evening. Just eight weeks to the day, since the street fight. The election for city marshal is only six days away. As Virgil proceeds from the Oriental saloon to his room at the Cosmopolitan Hotel. it is a half-hour before midnight.

His calf-wound has all but healed and he walks with just the trace of a limp. As the U.S. Deputy Marshal reaches the middle of the crossing of Fifth Street, shotgun blasts pour forth from a construction site on the southeast corner of the intersection. Two of the shots "take effect on Mr. Earp," but he does not lose his feet. The *Daily Epitaph* of the next morning comments, "It is simply a miracle that Mr. Earp was not instantly killed, as in the darkness, with the simple aid of a lighted paper the marks of nineteen shot were found on the east side of the Eagle Brewery and in the awning posts, three of them passing through the first window on that side of the

house."

The newspaper goes on to report that: "Mr. Earp walked back into the Oriental and told his brother, Wyatt, that he was shot. His friends escorted him to his room in the Cosmopolitan Hotel, and Dr. Mathews and Goodfellow were immediately called to attend upon him. It was learned before going to press that his left arm received the principal damage, the shot taking effect just above the elbow, producing a longitudinal fracture of the humerus, or bone between the shoulder and elbow."

George Parsons writes in his diary that : "Doc G [Goodfellow] had just left [Parson's room] and I tho't (sic) couldn't have crossed the street—when four shots were fired in quick succession from very heavily charged guns, making a terrible noise and I tho't were fired under my window under which I quickly dropped, keeping the dobe

[adobe] wall between me and the outside till the fusillade was over." Parsons goes on to rail at the "cowardly apathetic guardians of the peace" who seemingly did nothing to apprehend the assassins. After Virgil is taken to his room, Parsons writes: "Van and I went to hospital for Doc and got various things. Hotel well guarded, so much so that I had trouble to get to Earps room. He was easy. Told him I was sorry for him. 'It's Hell, isn't it!' Said he. His wife was troubled, 'Never mind, I've got one arm left to hug you with,' he said." Parsons ends his diary entry of Dec. 28 with the casual notation "Later we stopped at Mr. Masseys and had a game of Euchre with Mess. Morehhouse and White."

December 29, 1881

Upon receiving news of Virgil Earp's injuries, Marshal Crawley Dake telegraphs United States Marshal Wyatt Earp and authorizes him to deputize a posse.

December 30,1881

Mayor Clum is in Washington, D.C. and the newspapers there cover Virgil's shooting, giving "extended telegraphic accounts of this cowardly attempt at midnight assassination."

January 3, 1882

It is election day in Tombstone but John Clum does not run for re-election. The reason he gives is that he is seeking a governmental appointment elsewhere but it is a political fact that his support has been eroded by his association with the Earps and the gunfight scandal. Within a few months he will sell his interests in Tombstone and leave.

Dave Neagle, who replaced Virgil on the ticket, is elected City Marshal. Would Virgil have won? We will never know.

January 4, 1882

George Hearst, the wealthy, mining baron of California and father of William Randolf, visits Tombstone. There are rumors that Hearst will be kidnapped so he hires Wyatt Earp as a bodyguard while he visits the district's mines.

January 15, 1882

Parsons: "Had a fine experience other day with Doc [Goodfellow] in the Dead House [Morgue]. In one box were remains of two poor fellows who were blown up on the Barlacomari (sic). Nothing human was recognizable but their boots. Boots—bones and flesh mixed with hair and pieces of clothing presented anything but a cheerful aspect."

January 17, 1882

Parsons: "Much blood in the air this afternoon. Ringo and Doc Holiday came nearly having it with pistols...bad time expected with the cow-boy leader and D. H. [Doc Holiday]. I passed them both not knowing blood was up. One with hand in breast pocket and the other probably ready. Earps just beyond. Crowded street and looked like another Battle. Police vigilant for once and both disarmed."

January 23, 1882

In the middle of the night, Parsons is routed out of bed to help get a horse for the posse going down to Charston to rearrest Johnny Ringo. On the 25th Parsons notes: "The Earps are out too on U.S. business and lively times are anticipated...At last the National Government is taking a hand in the matter of our trouble and by private information I know that no money nor trouble will be spared to cower the lawless element. Our salvation, I think, is near at hand. It looks like business now when the U.S. Marshal [Crawley] Dake takes a hand under special orders."

The Earp posse combs the Charleston area looking for "Ringold" but they can't flush him out. The volunteers go back to Tombstone, but Earp and his men stay on the trail for a week. When they get back to Tombstone, they find out that Ringo has given himself up to Behan and is in jail awaiting trial.

February 4, 1882

Parsons: "People suspicious on roads. Every stranger I met mounted was cause for me to remove gauntlet so I could handle pistol freely."

February 9, 1882

Ike Clanton files his second murder charge against the Earps, this time with Magistrate J.B. Smith at Contention City.

February 15, 1882

Parsons: "Weather rainy and very disagreeable…Yesterday Earps were taken to Contention to be tried for killing of Clanton. Quite a posse went out. Many of Earp's friends accompanied armed to the teeth. They came back later in day, the good people below beseeching them to leave and try case here. A bad time is expected again in town at any time. Earps on one side of street with their friends and Ike Clanton and Ringo with theirs on the other side—watching each other. Blood will surely come. Hope no innocents will be killed."

Doing everything possible, Ike Clanton files his third murder charge against the Earps with Judge Lucas of Tombstone.

February 18, 1882

Parsons: "Another killing by Indians reported at Antelope Springs."

February 22, 1882

Parsons: "Celebrated day by going to Contention City horseback—quite a party of us for ride and to see the [railroad] cars, it being a little more than two years since I had seen a steam engine—locomotive—cars and track."

February 24, 1882

Parsons: "Small pox at last here after traveling over the east. Was vaccinated today."

March 4, 1882

Parsons: "Pleasant day. Coyotes singing as I write this in my cabin tonight. They are being pushed out from us though and would that the thieves and swindlers here could keep them company."

March 18, 1882

There is an "entertainment" at Schieffelin Hall. According to Mayor Clum, himself, Wyatt and Morgan, each had "concealed about our person an approved "45" six-shooter." The entertainment is the Lingard troupe and they are performing "Stolen Kisses."

Afterwards, Wyatt and Morgan retire to Campbell and Hatch's Saloon for a game of pool. As Morgan leans forward to make a difficult shot the upper window in the rear door is "splintered by tongues of flame and spitting lead."

There are two shots. The second bullet bores into the wall above Wyatt Earp's head. The first strikes Morgan Earp in the small

of the back, shattering his spine, and passing through his body. It keeps going and lodges in the thigh of George Berry standing by a stove at the front of the hall.

Before he dies, Morgan asks Wyatt to come close and he whispers something in his ear. Most present speculated Morgan requested a vow of vengeance. It would be quite a few years before Wyatt would reveal what his younger brother's last words really were.

March 19, 1882

Bells of Tombstone toll all day while Morgan Earp lays in state blanketed by flowers in the Cosmopolitan Hotel.

Parsons writes in his journal about the murder of Morgan: "Another assassination last night about eleven o'clock. I heard the shots, two in number, but hearing so many after dark was not particularly startled, though I remarked to Redfern about it. Poor Morgan was shot through by an unknown party. Probably two or three in number, in Campbell and Hatch's while playing pool with Hatch. The shots, two, came through the ground window leading into alley running to Fremont St.—on east side of Otis' & Co's store. Geo Berry received the spent ball in his thigh, sustaining a flesh wound. The second shot was fired apparently at Wyatt Earp. Murders (sic) got away of course, but it was and is quite evident who committed the deed. The man was Stilwell in all probability. For two cowardly, sneaking attempts at muder, this and the shots at Virgil E. when I came nearly getting a dose, rank at the head. Morg lived about forty minutes after being shot and died without a murmer. Bad times ahead now. Attended church, morning."

March 20, 1882

Wyatt accompanies Virgil and the wives to catch the train for California. Morgan's body has been sent the previous day.

Accompanying the U.S. Deputy are Doc Holliday, Warren Earp, Texas Jack, Sherm McMasters, Turkey Creek Johnson, all heavily

TUCSON PANORAMA, 1882

This magnificent view of the Tucson valley was taken from the Tucson Mountains looking northeast towards the Santa Catalinas and Redington Pass. This is the same pass Wyatt Earp and his posse came across in their marathon chase after Leonard, Crane and Head the previous year. At the time this photo was taken, Tucson was being rivaled by Tombstone for the claim of being the largest community in the territory, a badge the "Old Pueblo" had worn proudly for the past 100 years.

The bottom view is a blow-up of the top photo and shows the heart of the downtown area where Wyatt Earp and his men spent two hours after the shooting of Stilwell, searching in vain for Ike Clanton. The train, just beyond the downtown, is near the depot where Wyatt shot Stilwell. The trail meandering off beyond is the road to Fort Lowell. In several years the University of Arizona will be built over there and the location will be severely criticized as being "way the Hell out in the country."

armed with shotguns and revolvers.

In Tucson, Wyatt guards the family as they get off the train to eat dinner.

As the entourage comes out on the platform to reboard the train, Wyatt spots Frank Stilwell and gives chase (Ike Clanton claims that he and Stilwell were approaching the train to meet a grand jury witness who was coming in. Wyatt claims Stilwell was there for an ambush.)

It is about 7 P.M. and the westbound train prepares to leave. As the whistle blows, Wyatt catches up to Frank Stilwell, who is running across the tracks about twenty yards in front of the engine. Earp tells him to halt or he'll get it in the back. Stilwell turns and grabs for the barrel of Wyatt's shotgun. As they struggle, Wyatt forces the gun down until the muzzle of the right barrel is just underneath Stilwell's heart. Wyatt never says a word.

"Morg!" Behan's deputy blurts out "Morg!"

Stilwell is obviously seeing triple.

Parsons writes: "Tonight came news of Frank Stilwell's body being found riddled with bullets and buckshot. A quick vengeance and a bad character sent to Hell where he will be the chief attraction until a few more accompany him."

VENGEANCE IS MINE

March 21, 1882

Six men, all carrying rifles enter through the rear door of the Cosmopolitan Hotel. Sheriff Behan is in the front office and he confronts Wyatt Earp.

"I want to see you," Behan says.

"You've seen me once too often," Wyatt replies.

The Earp party, having flagged down a freight train outside of Tucson the night before (the engineer was not happy about it), rode the rails back to Contention where they retrieved their horses.

Wyatt is in a precarious position. Crawley Dake has given him official sanction and $2,600 to go after the cow-boys but the cold-blooded killing of Frank Stilwell has placed Earp outside the pale of the law. He will have to stand trial for murder or leave the country. He might be acquitted but he might also go to the penitentiary—or the gallows.

A telegram from Tucson arrives at 1 P.M.ordering sheriff Behan to arrest Wyatt for murder. The telegraph operator alerts Wyatt, who is a friend, and holds the missive for an hour. Wyatt tries to tie up as many loose strings as he can—liquidating his assets—and says good-bye to his friends.

March 22, 1882

Last night, Wyatt and his men went into camp about two miles north of Tombstone. This morning, a member of the Vigilante Committee sends Wyatt a copy of the final verdict of the

THE VENDETTA RIDE

Wyatt carries a pocketful of warrants for various criminals, but he crisscrosses the Tombstone hills specifically looking for anyone who had anything to do with the killing of his favorite brother. It will be his everlasting regret that he only got half the job done. This, in fact, is the motivation for Wyatt's later claim he killed Johnny Ringo, a deed many historians find implausible.

"If you are patient in one moment of anger, you will escape a hundred days of sorrow."
—OLD VAQUERO SAYING

coroner's jury which found that Morgan Earp came to his death at the hands of Peter Spence, Frank Stilwell, 'John Doe' Fries, a half-breed Indian known as Florentino Cruz, or Indian Charlie; and another halfbreed, Hank Swilling.

At about 11 A.M. Wyatt Earp and his posse ride into Pete Spence's wood camp in the South Pass of the Dragoons. They are informed by T.D. Judah that Pete is in Tombstone but that a half-breed named Florentino is looking for stock just beyond the camp. Earp and his men ride over the hill and pass out of view.

"A few minutes later," Judah reported, "I heard ten or twelve shots." The next morning when Florentino does not return, Judah proceeds in search of him and finds the body, riddled with bullets.

Years later, Wyatt will reveal that when he questioned Florentino, the half-breed admitted being paid $25 for watching the horses the night Morgan was killed.

"That twenty-five-dollar business just about burned me up," Wyatt said. The U.S. marshal also told a story about how he gave the half-breed a chance to draw by counting to three in Spanish. It is doubtful Wyatt gave him anything but a lead facial.

While Wyatt is in the South Pass, Behan is putting together a posse to go after the Earps. Down from Tucson, Pima County Sheriff, Bob Paul, refuses to join the posse when he sees who will ride against Wyatt. Ike Clanton, Phin Clanton and Johnny Ringo, all sworn enemies of the Earps are among the eager posse members. Paul demurs saying, "I'll let Wyatt know I want him, and he'll come in." As to Behan's posse, Paul says, "He persists in cloaking the most notorious outlaws and murderers in Arizona with the authority of the law. I will have nothing to do with such a gang."

March 23, 1882

Wyatt's gang has returned from Spence's camp and while he and his men wait near the old powder-house at the east edge of Tombstone, Texas Jack goes into town to arrange for one thousand dollars to be sent to Earp at Iron Springs, where he proposes to camp while riding the Babocomari wilderness looking for Curly Bill.

After a 25 mile ride and about five miles from Iron Springs, Wyatt leaves Warren to wait for the money to be delivered by one of the Vigilante messengers.

Wyatt and the rest push on to the springs to make camp. It is hot and the men and horses are tired. They see no sign of others using the trail so Wyatt loosens the gunbelts around his waist.

Fifty feet from the springs, intuition brings Wyatt up short. He swings out of the saddle, loops the reins in his left hand, and with the shotgun in his right hand, walks forward. Texas Jack and Sherm McMasters, still mounted, remain behind him, Holliday and Johnson, much further to the rear.

Another step gives Wyatt a full view of the hollow. Two men jump to their feet. One of them is Curly Bill and the other is Pony Deal. Curly stands to fight but Deal heads for the cottonwoods. Seven other rustlers explode out of the flimsy line shack and head for the timber. Wyatt waists no time and squeezes both triggers of his shotgun. Eighteen buckshot, a double load from Wyatt's Wells-Fargo gun strikes Curly Bill just beneath the chest wall, all but cutting his body in two.

As the rustlers open up from the cottonwoods with their pistols, Texas Jack's horse is shot from under him as all of Wyatt's supporters flee. Wyatt said that "Every mother's son, including my old pal Doc Holliday, one of the bravest men I ever knew, had turned tail at the first volley and

gone scampering into the distance as fast as their horses could run." Meanwhile, Wyatt is trying to remount his horse, but his loose gunbelt has slipped down off his hips which effectively prohibits him from forking his horse. As he struggles, a pistol shot takes off the saddlehorn.

"If you get my position," Wyatt explained to his biographer Stuart Lake, "You'll understand that my nose was almost touching the tip of the saddlehorn. I thought someone had struck a match on the end of it—my nose—I mean, and I smelled a very rotten egg."

The *Nugget* smelled a rotten egg too when they got the news of the fight at Burleigh Springs (the fight was deliberately misnamed as to location by the *Epitaph* to throw off Behan) The cow-boy newspaper offered a $100 reward for conclusive evidence of the death of Curly Bill. The *Epitaph* countered by offering to pay $2,000 to any worthy charity provided that Curly Bill would put in an appearance alive and well.

March 27, 1882

The Earp party reaches Henry Clay Hooker's ranch north of Wilcox. They ask for refreshments for themselves and their horses and are graciously treated to the famous Hooker hospitality. Wyatt and his men leave at about 7 in the evening and go into camp five miles from Eureka Springs.

March 28, 1882

Behan's posse reaches Hooker's ranch and demands refreshments. The sheriff asks Henry if he knows the whereabouts of the Earps. Hooker replies that he doesn't and that if he did he wouldn't tell him. Behan accuses Hooker of "upholding murderers and outlaws."

Hooker explodes. "I know the Earps and I know you and I know they have always treated me like a gentlemen; damn such laws and damn you, and damn your posse;

they are a set of horse thieves and outlaws."

Ike Clanton resembled that remark and he takes offense. "Damn the Son of a Bitch, he knows where they are and let's make him tell."

Hooker's foreman steps away and returns with a Winchester which he cocks and points at Mr. Honest Granger's head. "You can't come here into a gentleman's yard and call him a Son of a Bitch! Now you skin it back! Skin it back!"

Witnesses don't relate whether Ike took it back but Hooker set a separate table for the "honest ranchers."

After breakfast Behan goes out to the stable and speaks to the foreman. Johnny takes a diamond-stud from his shirt and says, "Take this, it cost a hundred dollars, but don't say anything about what occurred here." Of course, the foreman did because this exchange was printed in the *Epitaph* which is where this account came from.

Wyatt decides it's time to leave the territory. He takes his men and heads for Silver City. They arrive there on Saturday evening, April 8, 1882.

Reports of more battles will fill the *Nugget* for weeks, each one ending with the death of Wyatt Earp. These eye-witness accounts will prove to be a tad premature.

April 1, 1882

The *Nugget* reports that when the Earp party rode into a ranch 12 miles north of Willcox, Doc Holliday was overheard saying to Wyatt Earp, "The steel saved you that time." The steel being a crude, bullet-proof vest, which Wyatt was rumored to be wearing at the fight at Mescal Springs. Years later, Wyatt laughed and said, "I wonder if they thought about how hot one of those things would be on the Arizona desert."

Governor Tritle arrives in Tombstone and finds that the Earps have left the country.

LEGALEZE, PA-LEASE!

The hand written records from the Tucson District Court indicting Wyatt Earp, et. al., for the murder of Frank Stilwell, contain a rather (even for the times) baroque version of legal writing. Example:

"Doc Holliday, Wyatt Earp, Warren Earp, Sherman McMasters and John Johnston are accused by the Grand Jury of the county of Pima and territory of Arizona on this oath by the indictments of the crime of murder committed as follows: that the said Doc Holliday at the city of Tucson in the said county of Pima on or about the 20th day of March, A.D. 1882 with force and arms in and upon the body of one Frank Stilwell then and there being then and there feloniously, wilfully and of his malice aforethought did make an assault and the said Doc Holliday a certain gun charged with gunpowder and leaden bullets which he, the said Doc Holliday, in the hands then and there had and held, then and there feloniously, wilfully and of his malice aforethought in and upon the body of him the said Frank Stilwell did discharge and shoot off giving to him the said Frank Stilwell then and there with the said gun so discharged and shot off as aforesaid in and upon the body of him the said Frank Stilwell a mortal wound of which said mortal wound he the said Frank Stilwell died instantly."

Ah, could you repeat that again, please?

GOVERNORS OF ARIZONA

May 1, 1882

John P. Clum sells the Tombstone Epitaph and leaves Tombstone.

May 25, 1882

Parsons: "It was a singularly acting fire. It seemed to, and actually did, go against the wind."

A third fire, in as many years, destroys all the business dwellings on Allen Street below Fifth down to Fourth on both sides of the street and flames sweep up Fourth Street and burn the Post Office at the corner of Fourth and Fremont, crosses Fourth and burns westward taking all the buildings including the Papago Cash Store, where the fire stops. Parsons calls it "a good $350,000 fire with about $250,000 insurance." He also suspects arson, specifically the cow-boy faction. By the 30th, the town is full of adjusters. Two weeks of Parson's mail are destroyed along with a pair of "buckskin pants" he left to be cut at Black's.

AFTERMATH

May 25, 1882

Yet another fire guts the business area of Tombstone. This one didn't slow down the richest camp in the territory any more than the others. First came the insurance adjusters and tents, and then came newer, bigger buildings in a matter of weeks. Note the O.K. Corral sign which survived the fire (for another view of the sign see page 58).

O.K. Corral sign

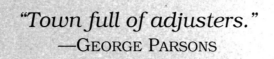

"Town full of adjusters."
—GEORGE PARSONS

THE RINGO MYSTERY
July 13, 1882

Several months after the Earps left Arizona, the cow-boy community is shocked by the death of Johnny Ringo.

Not far from Rustler's Park, Ringo's body is found sitting in the center of five large black jack oaks growing up in a semi-circle from one root. His watch is still running and his revolver is caught in the chain with only one shot discharged from it. He has a bullet hole in the head with a piece of scalp missing. His boots are gone and he had evidently taken off his undershirt and torn it in two, and wrapped it around his feet.

Buckskin Frank Leslie tries to take credit for Ringo's death and so does Wyatt Earp who claims he came all the way down from Colorado to do it.

Ringo's death is officially listed as a suicide and remains one of the stranger mysteries of the west.

JOHN RINGO

LEADVILLE, COLORADO 1885

May 22, 1882

Doc Holliday is arrested in Denver. He comments, "If I am taken back to Arizona, that is the last of Holliday."

In Gunnison, Colorado, Wyatt, sends for Josie who is home in San Francisco

As to his wife, there is no evidence that he ever contacted Mattie again. Speculation is that his wife travelled to Colton with the Earp family, and then waited in vain for Wyatt to send for her. When he didn't, she sheepishly made excuses for him as long as she could, finally leaving to join Katherine Holliday in Globe, Arizona. From there it is a one-way ticket down, as we shall see.

June, 1882

Arizona authorities try to extradite Wyatt and Holliday back to Arizona to stand charges for murder. Fearing they will be murdered,or at least convinced of that possibility, the governor of Colorado declines.

Doc now divides his time between Denver and Pueblo.

August 10, 1882

Virgil Earp is arrested in San Francisco on a charge of dealing faro. Over $1,000 and a "lay out" is captured with him.

December, 1882

The city hall and the Cochise County Courthouse are completed. The population now stands at 10,000, making Tombstone the largest town in the territory. The mines are at a peak and the growing metropolis brags that it is the brightest star between Denver and San Francisco.

LEADVILLE, COLORADO, 1885

Doc Holliday and Wyatt have a falling out and Doc gravitates to Leadville, Colorado, (left). From there he moves to Glenwood Springs where he hopes the mineral baths will cure his worsening tuberculosis. It is not to be.

DOC'S FINAL DISAPPEARING ACT
The mesa south of Glenwood Springs, Colorado where Doc Holliday is supposedly buried—he isn't.

Holliday's grave marker

May 19, 1883
John Behan is indicted on a misdemeanor charge of collecting taxes after his term expired.

Spring, 1884
Wyatt is in Eagle, Idaho where he is accused of claim jumping. He and his brother Jim also operate the White Elephant saloon in Eagle.

April 13, 1884
Will McLaury writes a letter to his father: "My experience out there [in Tombstone] has been very unfortunate as to my health and badly injured me as to money matters—and none of the results have been satisfactory. The only result is the death of Morgan and the crippling of Virgil Earp and death of McMasters..."

August 5, 1884
The cornerstone for the Statue

THE HOTEL GLENWOOD
Where Doc Holiday died.

of Liberty is laid on Bedloe's Island in New York.

1885
Water begins to hamper ore extraction in the mines catacombing the ground beneath Tombstone.

May 3, 1887
A devastating earthquake rocks northern Mexico and southern Arizona. Severe aftershocks level buildings in Tucson and cause structural damage to San Xavier Mission. The epicenter is located at Batepito, south of the border. In Bavispe, Mexico, not a single house is left standing and 47 people perish. The resulting buckling of the earth's plates under the surface of Goose Flats exposes the Tombstone mines to dramatic flooding. By 1897, the mines are all but shut down and there are only sixteen businesses left in Tombstone.

July 11, 1887
Virgil Earp is elected City Marshal of Colton, California. He is also sporting a gold badge recently presented to him by Wells Fargo for services done at Tombstone years earlier. The local paper says "It is a beauty and cost in the neighborhood of eighty dollars."
Part of the new Marshal's

duties are to "keep watch of the electric lights and note their burning."

September 14, 1887
Ike Clanton is shot and killed by a correspondence school detective at Peg Leg Wison's cabin on Eagle Creek, in eastern Arizona. He was running away at the time.

November 8, 1887
Doc Holliday dies about 10 A.M. in Glenwood Springs, Colorado. He had gone there hoping for a cure in the much touted natural, hot springs, steam baths and sanitarium. His last words are, "This is funny," which he says as he looks down at the end of the bed and sees that he's about to die with his boots off. The hearse taking his body to the local cemetery atop the mesa south of town, could not make it up the road because of the winter weather. As the years go by, Glenwood Springs grows outward and today, Doc lies buried in someone's backyard at the base of the mesa. The exact location is a closely guarded secret among the townspeople, for obvious reasons.

July 31, 1893
Shredded Wheat is patented by Henry Perky.

Mrs. Katherine Holliday and Mrs. Wyatt Earp get ready to entertain "guests" in Globe, Arizona. The two will soon wear out their welcome and Mrs. Earp will move on to Pinal, Arizona.

July 8, 1888

Virgil purchases a new house in Colton. In the county register of Deeds he writes: "I Virgil W. Earp, of the City of Colton, County of San Bernardino and State of California, for and in consideration of the love and affection which I bear towards my wife, and as an expression of my heartfelt gratitude to her for her constant, patient and heroic attendance at my bedside while I lay dangerously wounded at Tombstone, Arizona, do grant unto my wife, Mrs. Alvira Earp, as her separate estate, all that real property situated in the City of Colton..."

November 4, 1893

Virgil and Allie, restless to the end, leave Colton and take up residence in the new boomtown of Vanderbilt, California [See map on page 113. Vanderbilt is just above Needles and close to the Nevada line].

Virgil builds a two-story building called "Earp's Hall." A report in the *Needles Eye* reports:

"There was a dance at Earp's hall this week. Everybody was there, and it exceeded all past events."

Virgil runs for constable of Needles Township but loses soundly.

December 27, 1894

Virgil and Allie sell out their Vanderbilt property and head for Cripple Creek, Colorado to join Wyatt who thinks they should open a saloon.

October 23, 1895

Continuing to ping pong across the West, Virgil and Allie decide to try Arizona again and return to Prescott where they rent a house. Virgil gets active in mining and invests in the Grizzly mine.

November 17, 1896

While working in the Grizzly, a sudden cave-in pins Virgil to the ground leaving him unconscious for several hours. He is rescued but suffers from injuries that include crushed ankles and feet, a dislocated hip, a severe facial cut and assorted body bruises.

Once again, Allie tends to her husband and nurses him back to semi-health [his age and his many wounds are taking their toll].

After several months, Virgil and Allie move out to Kirkland Valley, southwest of Prescott. He raises horses and hogs. Showing his true stubbornness, Virgil goes back to working the Grizzly, hoping to strike it rich.

The bonanza doesn't happen and they spend the coming winter in Prescott where Virgil works as a deputy.

Fall, 1898

Virgil receives a letter from a woman in Portland, Oregon. The writer has read of the famous Virgil Earp and wonders if he is the same Earp who had married Ellen Rysdam in 1860. If so, the writer explains, she is Virgil's daughter.

This is a tumultuous moment. Virgil has always wanted children but Allie has been unable to conceive. Allie takes it in stride and comments that " for the first time in his life, Virgil finds out he has a grown-up lady daughter, Jane!"

Early in 1899, Virgil and Allie travel to Portland, Oregon by train to meet Jane and Virgil's ex-wife Ellen. Virgil and his daughter sit up late every night for the entire visit as father and daughter catch up on each others lives.

VIRGIL AND NIECES,
DATE UNKNOWN

WYATT & VIRGIL IN SAN DIEGO

1885–90

The two Earp brothers and their wives spend several years off and on in the San Diego area. Virgil owns two different saloons while here. Wyatt supposedly sells real estate, races horses and gambles.

The most famous photo of Wyatt (right) is taken during his stay here.

VIGRIL EARP, DATE UNKNOWN
This is how Virgil (below) looked after Tombstone. His left arm hangs, useless but the fire is still in the eyes.

DOWNTOWN SAN DIEGO, 1915

DEATH ON THE LINE

July 4, 1888

"My name is Frank Beeler. I am 65 years of age. I am a laborer and live in Pinal, Arizona."

Nervous and figity, Frank Beeler faces the Pinal coroner, W.H. Burson, who directs the inquest.

Coroner: "State to the jury all that you know about the cause of the death of the deceased."

Beeler: "The woman felt sick and I knew pretty well what the sickness was as I had waited on her once before when she was the same way. I went to her room here in Pinal day before yesterday and looked in the door. I asked her if she wanted anything. She was lying in bed and a man was lying there on the bed beside her. She said come in here and sit down I want to talk to you. I went in and sat down and she said she didn't feel well and pointed around beside to the stand to a beer bottle that stood there. I took the bottle out. It contained whiskey about one fourth full. And she and I drank it up. She said then that she wanted to get more whiskey and some opium or laudanum as she wanted to try and get some sleep. She said I would like to have you go to Luedke's and get me some laudanum as I cannot sleep. She then said go to Werners' and get some more whiskey. I went there and got fifty cents worth of whiskey and took it to her. Then she wanted me to go and get the laudanum. I went to Luedke and he gave me a small bottle of laudanum and I took it to her. I was away about two hours and then went back and saw a number of persons there. The Dr. was one of them and seemed to be trying to restore her. The Dr. asked me if there was any whiskey there.

Coroner: "Were you sober during the day yesterday?"

Beeler: "I can't say that I was, though I was able to attend to business."

Coroner "Wasn't you drunk in the afternoon?"

Beeler: "I was, but I didn't give her any laudanum when I was drunk."

The next witness, being duly sworn on his oath, says: "My name is T.J. Flannery. I am 30 years of age. I reside in Pinal, Arizona, occupation laborer."

Coroner: "State to the jury all that you know about the cause of death of the deceased."

Flannery: " I went in and saw by the position that she was lying in that something was wrong. I lit a light and went up to the bed and looked at her and her arms and face were covered with black spots. I suppose she had been taking more laudanum and had taken too much and was dead or dying. I felt her pulse and found they weren't beating. I asked Beeler what she had been taking and he said he poured her some laudanum and she had taken the whole bottle.

Coroner: "What is the name of the deceased, if you know?"

Flannery: "Mattie Earp."

The witness signs his name and then is recalled for one last question:

Coroner: "Did you hear the deceased threaten her own life?"

Flannery: "I have. Earp, she said, had wrecked her life by deserting her and she didn't want to live."

SAN FRANCISCO, 1906
WYATT'S FAVORITE CITY

FRISKY IN FRISCO

From 1890 to 1897 Wyatt and Josie live with relatives in and around the Bay area. In 1893 Wyatt is listed as a "capitalist" and resides at 145 Ellis Street. In 1895 his residence is 720 McAllister where his wife's sister lives.

By 1896, Wyatt is living at 514-A 7th Avenue near Fulton. He lists himself as a "horseman" in the 1896 directory and is, in fact, harness racing on the California circuit.

Wyatt's first trotting horse, Otto Rex, comes to him in a poker game in San Diego. The horseman now prefers spats and a derby (see caricatures on pages 100–101). He keeps his horses stabled at 514 7th Avenue in San Francisco.

In the summer of 1896, Wyatt sells two articles to the *San Francisco Examiner Sunday Magazine.* The first one is a florid explanation of those 27 seconds in Tombstone.

WYATT EARP, 48
Horseman and capitalist

WHERE THERE'S SMOKE...
Josie claims that the San Francisco earthquake (top) destroyed her marriage records—how conveeeeenient. Meanwhile, in Tombstone, Fly's photo gallery (above) burns to the ground in 1898 destroying many significant images of the early camp. However, this photo is the earliest known view of the gunfight site. Wyatt (left) is now in his late forties and tries to pass himself off as owner of a string of Trotters. He's not, he's on commission, and a woman from Santa Rosa actually owns the ponies.

WYATT EARP, WHOSE DECISION MEANT $10,000.

A FOUL TO REMEMBER

December 2, 1896

Wyatt is an odd man. If you'll remember way back in Tombstone, he wasn't heeled on the night when Curly Bill shot Marshal White. Then why would Wyatt referee a fight in San Francisco with a Colt .45 in his pants? Well, he did and claimed the reason is that he had a few enemies. Not nearly as many as he will have after tonight.

The famed Ruby Bob Fitzsimmons is going to box an upstart sailer named Tom Sharkey. There's only one problem—they can't agree on a referee. At noon, on the day of the fight, Earp is offered the job. Almost immediately, trouble brews when Fitzsimmon's manager hears that Earp is fixed.

The crowd at the Mechanic's Pavilion is growing impatient. Against his manager's advice Fitz decides to go ahead. When Wyatt is announced as referee, he steps into the ring and takes off his coat. To the astonishment of the crowd he's packing a .45 in his pants. He is disarmed (see next page) and thus holds the dubious distinction of being the only referee in California boxing history to be disarmed before a match can begin.

The fight goes well until the eighth round when Fitzsimmons knocks Sharkey to the canvas with a knockout punch. Earp calls a foul and gives the fight to Sharkey, who has to be carried from the ring.

Earp, 48, is eventually exonerated in court (Fitz sued for the purse) when he takes the stand to defend his controversial decision. He says, "I am a pretty close observer, and under most conditions I think I am cool. I went into the ring as referee to give a square decision and, so far as my conscience speaks, I have done so...I am very sure that Bat Masterson lost a great deal of money on this fight, but I have always been able to decide against my own money, and my friends can stand the consequences of such a decision."

Maybe his friends can, but the city of San Francisco cannot and the papers go wild for weeks—see for yourself on the next two pages.

WYATT IS DISARMED

San Francisco Examiner, Dec. 4, 1896

THE BRAWL AFTER THE FALL

Wyatt Earp received more publicity and newspaper coverage as the referee of the infamous Sharkey-Fitzsimmons prizefight than from all of his exploits in Kansas and Arizona combined. Three San Francisco newspapers ran articles about him and the fight almost everyday for a month. On this page is a sampling of some of those caricatures which give a fascinating insight into the West's most famous "lawman."

REFEREE EARP

San Francisco Call, Dec. 3, 1896

The only drawing which shows Wyatt Earp in the ring. *San Francisco Examiner, Dec. 3, 1896.*

"FITZ"   "TOM"

San Francisco Call, Dec. 12, 1896

San Francisco Chronicle, Dec. 4, 1896

Trainer Needham Illustrates, in Sharkey's behalf, the Australian's last three blows.

Fitzsimmons denies the foul and illustrates his last three blows in the contest.
San Francisco Examiner

Referee Wyatt Earp, who gave
Sharkey the Decision.
San Francisco Chronicle, Dec 3, 1896

Wyatt Earp on the witness stand, confessing
that his lively career has not brought him a
fortune. *San Francisco Chronicle*, Dec 9, 1896

San Francisco Cal, Dec 18, 1896

San Francisco Call, Dec 15, 1896

December 20, 1896

Wyatt is so disgusted by the notoriety from the fight that he liquidates his sporting assets and lives for two years without other employment.

March 17, 1897

Bob Fitzsimmons takes the World Heavy-weight Boxing crown from James J. Corbett in Carson City, Nevada. Wyatt and Bat Masterson are hired as part of a large force of bouncers. Wyatt is not asked to referee.

July 15, 1897

The *S.S. Excelsior* reaches San Francisco with a ton of gold. The rush is on for Alaska. Rumors of nuggets growing on bushes reach Wyatt and Josie in Yuma, Arizona. Wyatt sells his Studebaker wagon. As they head for San Francisco on the train, all they hear is "Gold!" and "Klondike!" Before Wyatt can outfit his expedition, he slips trying to catch a trolley car and badly dislocates his shoulder. He's bedridden for three weeks.

Finally, Wyatt and Josie leave San Francisco on the *S.S. City of Seattle* and head for the Alaskan goldrush. They can't reach Dawson as winter sets in so they stay in Rampart City through the winter of 1898–99.

July, 1899

Wyatt manages a "canteen" on Saint Michael. There are only two items in the place—beer at a dollar a drink and cigars at fifty cents each. Wyatt is managing for a percentage (10% off the top) and he is making $200 per day, seven days a week. He is 51.

September, 1899

Wyatt and C.E. Hoxsie build the Dexter Saloon in Nome, Alaska. When Wyatt cashes out two years later, he will make $85,000.

February 1, 1902

Wyatt shows up in Tonapah, Nevada.

WYATT EARP'S NORTHERN SALOON, TONAPAH, NEVADA, 1902

A friend named Al Martin actually ran the saloon, while Wyatt and Josie prospected

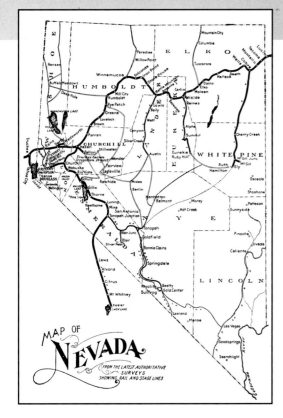

MAP OF **NEVADA**
FROM THE LATEST AUTHORITATIVE SURVEYS SHOWING RAIL AND STAGE LINES

Summer, 1904

Virgil and Allie keep their Colton home, but head out for the bonanza camp of Goldfield, Nevada. However, big money is in town and Virgil can't get in the game.

February 5, 1905

The *Tonapah Sun* reports that "Verge (sic) Earp, a brother of Wyatt and one of the famous family of gunologists, is acting as deputy sheriff [bouncer] in the National Club, Goldfield. Verge is a mild looking individual and to outward view presents none of the characteristics that have made the family name a familiar one in the west and in all the bonanza camps of the country from Mexico to Alaska."

"Virgil was a desert rat. I was just a desert mouse."
—ALLIE EARP

NEVADA BOOMTOWNS, 1905

Wyatt arrived in the new boomtown of Tonapah (top right) in January of 1902. He was fresh from his Alaska adventure and no doubt had some capital to invest. He went with what he knew— saloons, and financed one (above). Virgil landed in Goldfield (bottom right) and shared the streets with a new contraption—automobiles.

October 19, 1905

Virgil has pneumonia which he caught during an epidemic that claims ten other lives in Goldfield. He is bedridden once more and Allie, again, stands by her man. Unfortunately, this time his condition deteriorates and he is taken to the hospital next to the Miners' Hall. Allie describes his last moments: "He said to me, 'get me a cigar.' Believing he was feeling better I did so. 'Now,' he said, 'put Hickie's [his grand-niece] last letter under my pillow, light my cigar, and stay here and hold my hand.'"

She did and he slipped away from her for the last time.

Allie has stood by Virgil for 32 years. She will live another 42 years and never remarry.

WYATT IN A MOVIE?

"He was a visitor to the set when I was directing Douglas Fairbanks in 'The Half-Breed.' As was the custom in those days, he was invited to join the party and mingle with our background action. I think there was a trial of some kind. A group of people demanded that the half-breed be sent out of town. In that group was Earp. He only stood there and nodded his head. Earp was a one-eyed old man in 1915, but he had been a real marshal in Tombstone, Arizona and he was as crooked as a three dollar bill. He and his brothers were racketeers. All of them. They shook people down. They did everything they could to get dough. But they had the badge and they had the gun and they won all the gunfights simply by shooting the man before he was told he was arrested. And so they were terrific heroes in the eyes of certain people When I knew him, he was no longer a marshal and there was no longer a West, and he couldn't be the symbol that he had been. He looked for what anybody would look for and the first person who got ahold of him said he was a natural for show business. Well he was, and he wasn't. Our suspicion, because of the people who came around the set with him, was that he was looking for a place in law and order. He would have loved to have been chief of police of Los Angeles, or the marshal of the county. I think he was timid about being photographed, about acting and pretending. He knew inside himself that he wasn't an actor and had nothing to offer. I remember he saw Fairbanks bouncing around in the trees.and said, 'Oh no, I'd not like to do that.' And I think, for that reason, he took one last look and left."

—ALLAN DWAN

IS IT WYATT OR NOT?

The idea of the real Wyatt Earp actually moving on film was too much for researcher Jeff Morey. He tracked down "The Half-breed" and fast-forwarded to the scene, below. Unfortunately, it doesn't appear to be Wyatt. It looks like Texas John Slaughter who was in fact sheriff of Tombstone in the late '80s. Could Dwan have mistaken one lawman for another? If so, scratch everything he says about Wyatt.

WYATT EARP

TEXAS JOHN SLAUGHTER

FRAME BLOWUP

BUSTED!

July, 1911
Wyatt Earp, Walter Scott and Edward Dean are arraigned in Los Angeles for operating a "bunco game." At the Justice Court hearing, Wyatt is absolved of complicity although he doesn't exactly exude innocence when he gives the arresting officer a phony name—William Stapp. The alleged scam occurred near the Hollenbeck Hotel, center of Second and Spring Streets, in downtown Los Angeles, which is run by A. Bilicke, who owned the Cosmopolitan Hotel in Tombstone. One of the men arrested with Wyatt, Walter Scott, later talks a rich easterner into building a castle out on the Mohave desert— Scottie's Castle.

WYATT (on right) **UNDER ARREST AT THE SPRING STREET PRECINCT.**

TEDDY GOOSES WYATT'S STOCK

1902

As President of the United States, Teddy Roosevelt avidly enjoys the exploits and company of western lawmen. He befriends many, including Pat Garrett, Bat Masterson and Fred Dodge (right.) One night, when the president is entertaining Bat Masterson, Teddy's press secretary, Stuart Lake, overhears the remark from Bat that the true West will never be known until Wyatt Earp talks.

After Masterson's death, Lake keeps thinking about the comment and finally decides to do something about it. Friends at the Arizona Historical Society put him in touch with Wyatt and he travels to California to meet the infamous lawman. What he finds is a monosyllabic, feeble old man who is unable to recall many names, dates or actual events in his life. Perfect.

Lake's manuscript is serialized in the *Saturday Evening Post* prior to being published in October of 1931. Wyatt never saw a word. He died before it appeared. It's probably for the best, because it's doubtful Wyatt would have recognized himself. Lake transformed the itinerant gambler into a mountain of virtue, who single-handed had cleaned up the entire frontier.

Fred Dodge (left of the president) *cracks up Teddy Roosevelt in this undated photo.*

FRED DODGE ON HIS RANCH IN TEXAS AROUND 1905.

Fred Dodge worked undercover for Wells Fargo during his stay in Tombstone. He was a staunch friend and supporter of Wyatt Earp and respected him immensely. However, Fred broke rank with Wyatt on two important points: Wyatt never killed Johnny Ringo and Doc Holliday was involved in the Benson stage robbery.

"WILD BILL HICKOK" STARRING W.S. HART
The first actor to appear in a film as Wyatt Earp is second from the left in the above photo. W. S. Hart, as Hickok is third from the right. What's fascinating is the very real possibility that Wyatt Earp, himself, who was acting as a consultant, is standing off-camera looking at this scene.

REFLECTIONS OF A LIFE ON THE FRONTIER
*Wyatt Earp gazes across the Colorado River towards
Arizona in 1925. He has lived 77 years on the frontier and
no doubt has plenty to reflect on.*

July 6, 1900

Warren Earp is shot to death in the Headquarter's Saloon in Willcox, Arizona by Johnny Boyette, a cow-boy. Earp had been knocking around between California and Arizona, finally settling in the Wilcox area around 1892. He was working for the Cattlemen's Association when he was killed. The particulars are vague but Warren allegedly threatened Boyette, who was subsequently quickly acquitted in the shooting.

July 23, 1903

The Ford Motor Company sells its first automobile in Detroit, Michigan. It's a two-cylinder job.

July 26, 1903

The first transcontinental automobile trip is completed, from San Francisco to New York, at an average of 175 miles a day.

August 1, 1903

Calamity Jane dies and is buried next to Wild Bill Hickok.

May, 1905

Wyatt discovers his "Happy Day" mines near Parker, Arizona.

1905

An engineer named John H. Flood Jr. is introduced to Wyatt Earp at the Hampton Arms in downtown Los Angeles.

Wyatt hopes the engineer can help him locate mining properties out on the Mojave desert.

Flood eventually assumes the responsibility of taking care of Wyatt's mines, his correspondence and finding residences for Wyatt and Josie. In short he becomes Wyatt's personal secretary (although he is never paid—he simply likes them.)

In time, Flood will attempt to write Wyatt's life story. There is only one problem—Flood is an engineer not a writer. The two try to shop the manuscript to book publishers but there are no takers. When Wyatt befriends the

JOSIE AND WYATT AT THEIR WINTER CAMP NEAR VIDAL, CALIFORNIA

movie star William S. Hart, the actor tries to help market the property. He even uses his pull and has a screenwriter help Flood with a rewrite. Still no takers.

One book editor calls it "diffuse." but most say it's just not very interesting.

How bad were Flood's efforts? Here's an example from the section on the gunfight:

"From the scattering few shots at the opening of the fight, the firing increased to a roar. Over the housetops came the tide, between the alleys and through the streets, the crashing and pounding reverberating against the walls of the buildings and magnified a thousand times, stirring the

"That feller Hamlet was a talkative man. He wouldn't have lasted long in Kansas."
—WYATT EARP, AFTER HAVING READ SHAKESPEARE

Every winter for over twenty years, Wyatt and Josie camped out and prospected around the Colorado River area. The photos on these two pages date from the early twenties.

WYATT AND "EARPIE"

minds of the populace to the wildest imaginings.

"Crack! Crack! Crack! Crack! Crack! Crack!

"Crack! Crack! Crack! Crack! Crack!"

[Jumping ahead now past dozens of "Cracks!"]"...So rapid were the flashes that the heat of the metal extended back into the butts of the forty-fives until the palms of the gunners began to burn.

"Smoke! Smoke! Smoke! Smoke that glided like a wisp, smoke that oozed, smoke that rose and fell; the vacant lot was full."

Well the vacant lot wasn't the only thing that was full—as you can tell, the manuscript was full of—Bull! Bull! Bull! [I went through and counted the number of "Cracks!" and counted 102. as in *102 shots fired!* This, of course is somewhat at variance with the testimony given at the Spicer hearing.

November 12, 1907

Nicholas Earp dies in the Soldier's Home at Sawtelle, California.

October 25, 1921

Bat Masterson dies while writing at his desk at the *Morning Telegraph* in New York. Stuart Lake realizes he must go out west and find Wyatt Earp before it is too late because it was Bat Masterson who said, "The real story of the Old West can never be told, unless Wyatt Earp will tell what he knows; and Wyatt will not talk."

January 25, 1926

James Earp dies in Los Angeles. His wife, Nellie Bartlett Ketchum whom he married in 1873, died in San Bernardino in 1887.

November, 1928

Wyatt, in spite of being sick, goes out to vote for Al Smith, a Catholic.

HELLDORADO

October 24–27, 1929

Tombstone celebrates its first Helldorado celebration. Oldtimers come from everywhere to relive the old days. The event's organizers want Wyatt Earp to come and re-enact the Johnny-Behind-the-Deuce standoff but someone informs them that Johnny died years ago. Wyatt won't make it either.

Much to the horror of many of the original residents, a mock gunfight, recreating the Earp-Clanton feud, is staged on Fremont Street. John Clum is not

JOHN CLUM

amused: "The mock street battle between the city police and the rustlers was a grim exhibition that should have been omitted. The spectacle of men engaged in mortal combat is repulsive and distressing. It is inconceivable that any normal spectator derived either pleasure or benefit from viewing the mock battle. The lamentable clash between the city police and the rustlers on October 26, 1881, occasioned more partisan bitterness than anything else that ever occurred in that community–and traces of that bitterness linger to this day. There was no justification for the inclusion of that gruesome act in the HELLDORADO program, and, in my judgement, the mock street fight was reprehensible—even from a HELLDORADO standpoint."

Old John can't see the forest for the trees. "Normal spectators" will receive both "pleasure" and "benefit" by viewing the "gruesome act" recreated for at least one century (and going on two).

HEAVEN AND HELL

"It is from politeness to my maker that I attend church at all here, where numbskulls and old broken down ministers have charge of spirituality."
—GEORGE PARSONS
AUGUST 14, 1881

GEORGE PARSONS, APRIL 7, 1929

Tombstone's diarist returns to the scene of the shrine. He lives in Los Angeles now where he is a movie censor for the city. How fitting for the man who attended two churches while in Tombstone. He is seen here standing in front of the Tombstone Episcopal Church, where he was baptized on February 24, 1884

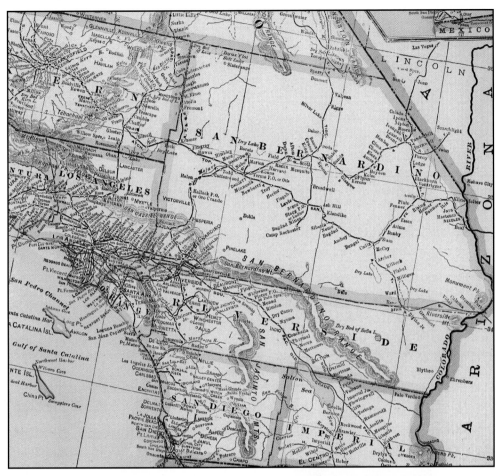

SAN BERNARDINO COUNTY, 1915

This map shows the stomping grounds of Wyatt Earp in his last years. He and his wife wintered in Los Angeles and then travelled through Colton out to their mines which were near Vidal, west of the Colorado River and Parker, Arizona. In 1930, California established a post office in the little desert town nearest to Wyatt's Happy Day group of mines. The settlement officially became Earp. A museum sprang up on the site and one of Wyatt's mine shacks was drug in for the tourists to see. Also shown is Vanderbilt, the town where Virgil lived briefly in the 1890s (it's northwest of Needles, California).

STILL CARD CRAZY
AFTER ALL THESE YEARS

Well into his seventies, Wyatt is still gambling heavily, hunting up card games wherever and whenever he can. He's gone from home days and even weeks at a time, hitting all the camps up and down the Colorado River, including Parker, Vanderbilt, Oatman, Goldroad, Chloride, Searchlight and White Hills.

JOSIE EARP
IN HER FIFTIES

"Braggin' saves advertisin'"
—SAM SLICK

TWO TALL TAILS

1928

Twenty three years have gone by since Wyatt Earp and John Flood first tried to sell their manuscript about Wyatt's life. Now, with the mood of the country changing, two writers rush to get out first with the his story. Walter Noble Burns had a runaway success with "The Saga of Billy the Kid" in 1926. He's looking to strike it rich with a new character and he thinks he has found him. Unfortunately, he's been beaten to the punch by Stuart Lake. Wyatt is committed to Lake as his biographer, and Burns publishes "Tombstone" without Earp's help.

The Truth of Morg's Last Words

For almost half a century the myth stands that Morgan Earp whispered a red oath to Wyatt when he died. Walter Noble Burns repeats it in his book "Tombstone": "' Bend down to me, Wyatt,' Morgan murmured. 'I'm dying.'

Walter Noble Burns

"Bending over him, Wyatt nodded his head grimly as the mortally wounded men whispered some secret in his ear."

Stuart Lake scoops Burns by including in his book "Wyatt Earp Frontier Marshal" what Morgan actually said.

Wyatt relates that "Morgan had a boyish curiosity which I never knew to be satisfied. He had been much interested in reported experiences of persons who were said to have had visions of heaven when at the point of death, and who had rallied long enough to leave behind them word of what they saw. Morg got me to read one of his books on this subject, and one night when he and I were camped on the desert, we had quite a discussion over it. I told him I thought the yarns were overdrawn, but at his suggestion we promised each other that, when the time came for one of us to go, that one would try to leave for the other some actual line on the truth of the book. I promptly forgot the thing. Morg didn't. He was sensitive to the fun others might poke at such notions, so, in the last few seconds of his life, when he knew he was going, he asked me to bend close.

"'I guess you were right, Wyatt,' he whispered, 'I can't see a damn thing.'

"That was all he said."

(l to r) WILLIAM S. HART, WYATT EARP AND TOM MIX

THREE HOMBRES

WILLIAM S. HART

William S. Hart and Tom Mix were two of the biggest cow-boy stars to ever gallop across a movie screen. It is fitting that they knew and admired Wyatt Earp.

Two of them had more in common than being legends. Wyatt and Tom Mix were both prone to "yarns" especially when recalling their past. Mix claimed to have been a Texas Ranger (among other lawman affiliations) and claimed service in the Spanish-American War, The Boxer War in China and the Boer War. There is no evidence he did any of the above.

What he did do was put people in movie seats. Mix started in films in 1909 and by the teens was making $10,000 a week (with no taxes taken out!).

William S. Hart got started later, in 1914, but during his time was just as big a star. He was also a writer and director and helped develop the Western's feature-length potential.

Wyatt hung out on their sets and gave them advice on authenticity (not that it was often followed, especially by Mix).

During a lean spell, Wyatt borrowed $50 from Hart.

Both men attended Wyatt's funeral as honorary pall bearers.

WYATT IN HIS RENTED BUNGALOW
The Earps stay in thirteen separate California addresses from 1920 to 1929, mostly tourist-type, light housekeeping bungalows like this one.

"The less you bet, the more you lose when you win."
—WYATT'S CREED

WYATT CASHES OUT

January 13, 1929

He couldn't stop.

He couldn't, or wouldn't, stop gambling. He had promised Josie many times that he would give it up but he was hooked on cards for life. And now, that life was in danger. The all night poker games had taken their toll on the 80-year-old man. Just two weeks ago he was out to all hours of the morning cutting the deck. Now, the fact is that what he can't stop, the body will.

John Clum makes his last call at the Earp's rented bungalow in downtown Los Angeles. He knows.

John Flood is there. He knows.

At about two o'clock Wyatt stirs and asks for water. As he drinks it he seems to think of something and as he hands the glass back to his wife he says to no one in particular, "Suppose..."

He repeats it. "Suppose."

At 8:05 a.m. on Sunday, January 13, 1929, the life of Wyatt Berry Stapp Earp ends.

His other life—the invented one, is just beginning.

HONORARY PALL BEARERS
(l-r) *W.J. Hunsaker (Wyatt's attorney in Tombstone and the "Dean of the Los Angeles Bar"), George Parsons, John Clum, William. S. Hart, Wilson Mizner and Tom Mix.*

"The frontier breeds men. Good or evil, law-abiding or lawless, the pick of the strain are fighting men."
—STUART LAKE

NO HALO

"So hail and farewell to the lion of Tombstone. Strong, bold, forceful, picturesque was this fighter of the old frontier. Something epic in him. Fashioned in Homereric mould. In his way, a hero. Whatever else he may have been, he was brave. Not even his enemies have sought to deny his splendid courage. The problems of his dangerous and difficult situation, he solved, whether wisely or foolishly, with largeness of soul and utter fearlessness. No halo is for this rugged, storm-beaten head. He was a hard man among hard men in a hard environment. What he did, he did. The record stands. But, weighed in the balance, he will not be found wanting. Judged by the circumstances of his career, the verdict in his case is clear—Wyatt Earp was a man."

—WALTER NOBLE BURNS

WYATT BERRY STAPP EARP
1848—1929
His last photo, taken two weeks before he died.

HASTA LA VISTA

"It is all hazy in my mind now."
—GEORGE PARSONS,
APRIL 15, 1925

As the Twentieth Century spreads out, Wyatt's world begins to crumble beneath the crush of progress. Slowly at first, and then with a mad rush, worthy of a new strike, the "oldtimers" begin to exit off the stage.

Josephine Sarah Marcus Earp—Wyatt called her Sadie (witness all the Earp wives with "Sporting" names, Allie, Bessie, Mattie, Deelie). Although there is no proof they were ever married, Sadie and Wyatt put up with each other for almost 50 years.

She outlived him by fifteen years—she died on December 19, 1944—and she considered it her dying mission to savagely attack anyone who tried to tell the true story of Wyatt Earp. She pretty much succeeded.

Albert Bilicke—Owner of the Cosmopolitan Hotel and eyewitness at the Spicer Hearing, Mr. Bilicke made his mark in Los Angeles with the world class Hollenback Hotel. He drowns on the Lusitania, in 1915.

Luke Short—Dies of Dropsy at Geuda Springs, Kansas on September 8, 1893.

John Behan—In spite of all the sniping by Earp aficionados, Behan's career certainly reads better than his ex-girlfriend's lover; Sheriff of both Yavapai and Cochise counties, representative in the Seventh and Tenth state assemblies from Prescott and Mohave county. He served as superintendent of the Territorial State Prison at Yuma from 1888 to 1890. He served with honor in the Spanish-American War and was a government "secret agent" in China during the Boxer

DEATH AND TAXES
By the late twenties, the Mining Exchange building (above), once the pride of Tombstone, is a leaning wreck. To avoid paying taxes on it the owner has it torn down.

Rebellion. His son, Albert became a law officer also. (Ironically, Sadie Earp was close to Albert all her life, having become attached to the boy when she lived with Johnny in Tombstone.) John Behan died at Tucson on June 12, 1912.

Bat Masterson—After his tumultuous tenure as a lawman,

THE GHOST IN THE TREE

Billy Breakendridge decides to write a book about his experiences in Tombstone. As he does research for what will become an anti-Earp tome called "Helldorado," he visits the site of Johnny Ringo's grave. A companion snaps a picture of Billy sitting in the bough of the tree where Ringo was found. When the film is developed an eerie face floats above the head of the aged lawman. Is it Ringo?

Bat turned sportswriter, writing his first article on horse racing on July 4, 1884. He married Emma Walters in 1891, moved to New York City in 1902 becoming a sports editor on the Morning Telegraph. There, he told a budding reporter, Stuart Lake, that the true story of the West would never be told until Wyatt Earp talked. Bat was a fixture at prize fights and sporting events and was the inspiration for the character Sky Masterson in Damon Runyon's "Guys & Dolls." He died at his desk, October 25, 1921 while writing about the poor getting ice in the winter and the rich getting it in the summer.

Billy Breakenridge—Another fine officer who has been smeared because of his alliance with Behan. In a letter to John Clum in the thirties, Fred Dodge wrote that "Billy was a nice young girl in those days, and undoubtedly today is a nice old lady."

The inference that Billy was gay has no bearing on his fine record as a lawman. He served under Behan for two years, served as deputy U.S. Marshal under W.K. Mead in Phoenix for nine years. In 1891 he was made special officer for the Southern Pacific Railroad and in all that time had "numerous unpleasant and highly exciting adventures, but never flinched from duty." He died in Tucson January 31, 1931.

Bob Fitzsimmons—had a long fight career, amassing an estate valued at $155,000. During his 34 year career he lost only one fight on a foul—the fight refereed by Wyatt Earp. He died of pneumonia in Chicago on October 22, 1917 at age 54. His fourth wife quickly went through his money and then asked the courts to allow her to dig him up so she could obtain the nine diamond fillings in his teeth. The request was denied.

TALL TALES ON THE SILVER SCREEN

The blazing pistols of Wyatt Earp have ripped through over twenty films.

He has been portrayed by Burt Lancaster, Henry Fonda (see right), James Garner, Walter Huston, Randolph Scott, Johnny Mack Brown, Richard Dix, Kurt Russell, Kevin Costner and Ronald Reagan. Even though Reagan only appeared in six westerns, he became identified totally with the genre. In the 1980 presidential race President Jimmy Carter solemnly reminded the American people that Reagan's arm control stance was reckless, adding "we are not dealing here with another shoot-out at the O.K. Corral."

HOUR OF THE GUN, 1967

James Garner (below) stars as Wyatt. Notice how Virgil is pushed behind Wyatt, who is singlehandedly taking everybody out.

MY DARLING CLEMENTINE, 1946

John Ford's take on the Earp-Clanton feud. Many writers have declared that even though it is wildly inaccurate regarding Wyatt and the gunfight, it is "how it should have been, not how it was." This is like saying that "The Wizard of Oz" is how Kansas should have been.

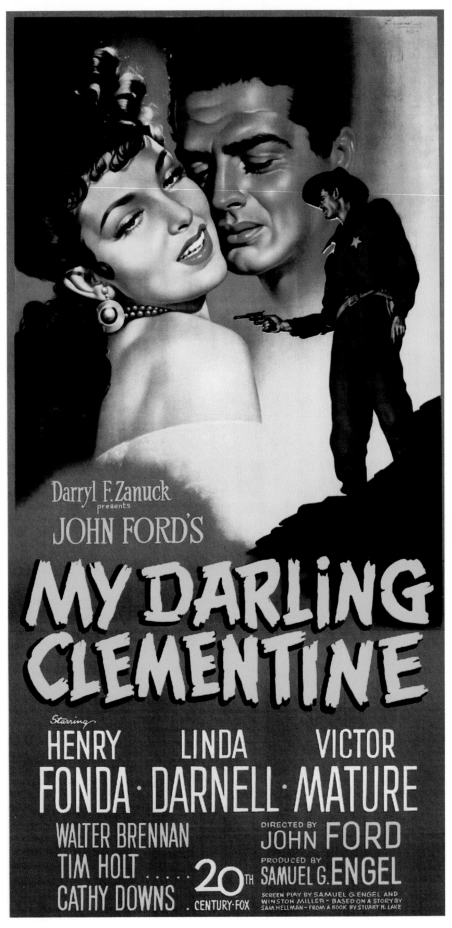

"All these books makin' him out a big hero are pure gingerbread."
—ALLIE EARP

August 2, 1939

Albert Einstein writes to Franklin D. Roosevelt and suggests that the atomic bomb is feasible.

August 6, 1945

A United States B-29 bomber called the "Enola Gay" drops the first wartime atomic bomb on Hiroshima, Japan. The 10-foot long weapon totally destroys 4.1 square miles of the city and kills over 100,000 people.

ADIOS ALLIE

November 17,1947

Twenty-one days before her hundredth birthday, Aunt Allie dies in Los Angeles. She has lived long enough to see her brother-in-law portrayed on the silver screen by the likes of Walter Houston, Joel McCrea, Randolph Scott and Henry Fonda. She pronounced them all as "gingerbread." To her, Virgil stood the tallest of the Earps and perhaps she was right. Only a handful of old-timers attend the funeral. There is no eulogy, only a tiny casket holding a bright-eyed lady from another era. Frank Waters writes an obituary, but no newspaper or magazine will print it. Waters sums up her long and remarkable life by stating that "in the great American Myth of westward expansion her campfires will glow across a thousand miles of mountain and plain, her blind faith and courage will keep the wagons rolling, her ready wit will shoot sharper than any six-shooter."

Outside, traffic moves through the encroaching smog.

"GUNSMOKE"

The second longest-running television series ever, is based on a composite of Wyatt Earp, Bat Masterson and several other Dodge City lawmen. The series began on radio in 1952 and then was developed for television .It premiered on CBS, September 10, 1955. The producers originally wanted John Wayne for the Matt Dillon part, but he turned them down and recommended a friend, James Arness, pictured here with Dennis Weaver, as Chester. The popular series ran until 1975. By the way, "60 Minutes" is the longest running series.

"Tombstone flames no more. Its wild days are a tale that is told. It lives with its memories and its ghosts. Sunshine and peace are its portion. Once it was romance. Now it's a town."

—WALTER NOBLE BURNS

WYATT ARRIVES FOR GOOD

1950s

Fueled by the movies,books and TV shows like "Gunsmoke," and "The Life and Legend of Wyatt Earp", the Lion of Tombstone finally reaches the pantheon of the great Western heroes. His frock-suited profile stands shoulder to shoulder with Wild Bill Hickok, George Armstrong Custer and Buffalo Bill. Interesting, considering that Wyatt was discovered after he died.

It is also more than a little ironic that the man who was never more than a deputy or an assistant marshal, would become the most famous Western lawman in American history. Think about it—in all his travels he couldn't even *get nominated* to run for sheriff, much less win. Compare

that fact with the following statement made by a marine commander landing in Somalia, "This may be Dodge City but we're Wyatt Earp."

As the fifties Earpamania reached its peak, many diligent researchers began to uncover the darker side of Wyatt's career—the wives, the arrests and the cons. In the 1960s, the public and the movies began to revise their image of Earp downward. It looked as if Wyatt might be headed for the ash heap of popular history. By the seventies, revisionist Westerns like "Doc" even went so far as to

CHILDREN'S BOOK. 1956
"Wyatt Earp"
by Philip Ketchum

WYATT AND MATTIE OUT OF THE CLOSET

portray Wyatt and Holliday as crooked homos.

For some reason, Wyatt's star only slid so far and then it stopped. Now, twenty years later, a new wave of Earp movies and books (like this one) are trotting out the trusty old gunfighter for a new ride. The same 27 seconds will be portrayed over and over, each one wildly different except for one thing—Wyatt Earp never gets a scratch.

AN IOWA FAMILY PHOTO ALBUM, 1953
The Town too tough to Die didn't die because of one man—Wyatt Earp. As John Gilchriese said, "Silver made Tombstone rich. Wyatt Earp made it famous." Because of him, thousands of tourists visit the town every year to see where he walked and where they stood during those 27 seconds.

DODGE CITY PEACE COMMISSION, 1883

Back Row (l to r) W. H. Harris, Luke Short, Bat Masterson, W.F. Petillon, Front Row (l to r) Charlie Bassett, Wyatt Earp, W. F. McLain, Neil Brown. The original photo above shows the boys to be smoking cigars. Also, it must have been a muddy day, check out the shoes. As Wyatt Earp's fame grew, writers and publishers began to monkey with this photo (see the grotesque example at left). Sometimes W. Petillon is edited out as shown here. In other versions, Bill Tilghman is added in. A vivid example of the distortion and cartooning of Wyatt's life.

HATS OFF

It seems obvious that the costume designers for the Wyatt Earp TV show got their inspiration for Wyatt's hat from Luke Short. (See opposite page)

Wyatt's hat

Luke Short's hat

*"Wyatt Earp,
Wyatt Earp,
Brave, courageous
And bold,
Long live his fame
And long live his glory
And long may his
story be told."*
—WYATT EARP TV THEME
SONG

THE LIFE AND LEGEND OF WYATT EARP
Actor Hugh O'Brian starts to draw his Buntline Special (he has a normal length gun, in his left holster). ABC premiered this "adult western" in 1955 and it ran for several seasons.

THE KID FROM TOMBSTONE

May 31, 1993

"Do you feel lucky, Dad?"

"Well, do you?"

I know, wrong movie, wrong genre, but the Kid from Tombstone doesn't care. He cares about the important stuff.

Behind him is Schieffelin Hall, the last standing building from the original Tombstone. The Kid from Tombstone doesn't care about that either. Beyond his back is Fourth and Fremont Streets where they actually walked. He sort of cares about that.

He doesn't care if Wyatt Earp wore a long coat or a short one, whether he was a deputy sheriff or a U.S. marshal. He doesn't care whether the Buntline Special was fact or fantasy, whether Wyatt cheated at cards or on his wife, or whether he threw a fight or faked a career.

He cares about the 27 seconds.

The Bad Guys against the Good Guys. Right against wrong. Yadda, yadda, It's as old as the hills and bound to get even older whether we tell him the truth, or not.

Somewhere, even as you read this, someone is carving up his enemies (I'm guessing Compton, California). Years from now, this unknown will emerge as a hero of our times. I can guarantee you one thing:

"You won't like him, he's not who you think he is."
—BOB BOZE BELL

"The fight of October 26, 1881, lasted less than a minute; its prelude twenty two months; its epilogue until this day."
—John D. Gilchriese

CREDIT

WHERE CREDIT IS DUE

*This book is dedicated to
William Heywood,
who helped me open the door,
and Jeff Morey,
who turned on the lights.*

DESIGN AND COMPUTER GRAPHICS
Dave Ritter

Additional computer design, Karen Stucke; **Edited by** Marianne Lasby; **Cover Lettering** Bob Steinhilber; **Historical Editing** by Bob Palmquist and Jeff Morey; **Tri Star Commercial Printing**, Chris Sicurella, Theresa Broniarczyk; **Suzanne Brown Art Galleries,** Suzanne Brown, Linda Corderman

MODELS
Wyatt, *Jeff Morey;* **Virgil**, *Richard Dobberstein, Paul Northrop;* **Morgan**, *Dan O'Connor;* **Doc,** *Gary Lehman, Bob McCubbin;*
Allie Earp, *Ruth Dixon;* **Mattie Earp**, *Debra Dodds (I forgot her name in the last book, so let's mention her one more time.) Debra Dodds;*
Globe Whores, *Jennie Smith & Miss Connie;* **Ike Clanton**, *Thunderbolt;* **Billy Clanton**, *Tony Tullis;* **Johnny Behan**, *Glenn Cummings;*
Billy Claiborne, *David Dixon;* **Frank McLaury**, *"Doc" Ingalls;* **Frank McLaury's horse**, *Penny, trained by Sandie Fendrick;*
Tom McLaury, *William Porter;* **Extras**, *Barbara Kemp, Kathy Lewis*

*10:42:07 a.m.
August 5, 1993.
Photo reference shot,
Pioneer Living
History Museum,
Pioneer, AZ.*

SPECIAL THANKS
*Laurie Williams and the Pioneer Living History Museum; Evelyn Cooper, Arizona Historical Foundation; Red River Leather; The Mercantile; My Lawyer Roxanna Bacon—thanks for getting that horsewoman off my back; Jerry Sanders and family; Paul Northrop and Outrider Tours; The Silver Lady Antiques; Lloyd and Jean Clark; Taplou Weir; Bobbi Guess Cady; Argonaut Book Shop; Scottsdale Booksellers; Guidon Books; Cappy Kirby; Jeff Dean; Jim Dunham; Jerry Weddle; John Brinkman, Dan Alexman, Foothills Photo; Gregg Clancy, Strawberry Fields—thanks for the bitchin' Billy the Kid and Wyatt Earp T-shirts!;
Jerry and Cleis Jordan of Casa de Patron—damn you guys sell the books!*

People Who Inspired Me
(to steal from them)
John Gilchriese, Frank Waters, Walter Noble Burns, Billy Breakenridge, Jack DeMattos, Stuart N. Lake, Al Turner, Glenn Boyer, John Myers Myers, William Shillingberg, Fred Dodge, Donald Chaput, Richard Erwin, and many others whose names I have forgotten (but I didn't forget to steal from)

REAL PHOTO CREDITS
There are many real photos in this book and I would like to thank the following individuals and organizations for allowing me to use their wonderful photos: Bob McCubbin for the use of the Josephine Marcus photo on page 8, plus the O.K. Corral and Spangenburg documents on page 68; Craig Fouts for the use of his original photos of Wyatt Earp on pages 3 and 124, and Bat Masterson, 25; The Arizona Historical Society for their fine collection, (At my request, the photo department reshot many of their photos to include the full card—they turned out great. Thanks!) including the photographs on pages 2, 26, 27, 34, 49, 51, 54, 69, 72, 85, 90, 91, 112 and 118; Dorothy McLaughlin for the photos on pages 18, 31; Jeff Morey for the photographs on pages 9, 38, 42, 43, 50, 106, 108, 109, 110, 111, 117, 118; Sharlott Hall Museum, 30, 31; Nevada State Historical Society, 102, 103 (both); Lee Silva, 104, 107, 116; Jack Burrows, 92, Jack DeMattos 100, 101, 128; Jim Earle 95, 96; Stephen and Marge Elliot 44, 80;Kansas Historical Society and Boot Hill Museum, 22, 24; Arizona Historical Foundation, 31 (both), 63.

Cartoon by Jimmy Swinnerton, 1896

Earpquake!

Bus stop, Thomas Road & Sixteenth Street, Phoenix, Arizona,
June 7, 1994.

THE MEDIA HAS BEEN GETTING IT WRONG FOR A LONG TIME

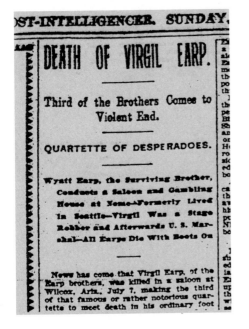

Sunday, July 22, 1900

The *Seattle Post Intelligencer* runs an article detailing the death of Virgil Earp (it was actually Warren). The source for most of the "Earp history" in the piece was copied from a news story written by a San Francisco sports writer who lost money on the Fitzsimmons-Sharkey fight. Perhaps as a direct result of this scandalous reporting, in September, Wyatt decides to set the record straight and write his memoirs. No doubt he was sick of the increasing distortions and outright lies being spread about himself and his brothers in newspaper coverage throughout the west. Here are some excerpts from the *Seattle-Post* article. (All spelling and punctuation has been left as is; bracket notations are the author's):

News has come that Virgil Earp of the Earp brothers, was killed in a saloon at Willcox, Ariz. July 7, making the third of that famous or rather notorious quartette to meet death in his ordinary footgear, after the traditional manner of the Western bad man. And a bad man was Virgil Earp. So were all the other Earps...All of them were gunfighters and men of prompt and bitter courage. Wyatt Earp is credited with ten men, one of them his own brother-in-law [Incredibly, this refers to Ike Clanton! At the most, Wyatt killed four men]...Every one of the Earps had killed his men-not man- and were famed in Tombstone, Ariz., and the Cochise country round about as qualified to pull and make a center shot in less than one-tenth of a second. They all filed the sights from their guns and shot by instinct rather than by aim. Triggers were a superfluous piece of mechanism and all were addicted to the process, in a fight, technically known as "fanning" their guns. By this means a man with a brace of Colts six-shooters becomes for the moment an animated machine gun.

The one of the Earps best known in Seattle was Wyatt, who refereed the Fitzsimmons-Sharkey fight [in San Francisco]. His connection with Seattle centers in the fact that not long ago he was the proprietor of the gambling house at 111 South Second. He was carried along by the Nome rush, however, and is now engaged in similar pursuits in that city.

Hot Times In Tombstone

In the early eighties the Earp family abode at Tombstone, Ariz., and did much toward making that hamlet a thrilling place of residence.

There were then two factions at Tombstone. Virgil and Wyatt Earp led one—the stage robbers; Johnny Behan, Ike Clanton and Jack Ringo [close], led the other—the rustlers. The stage robbers were in politics Republican and stood up stages and plundered express companies for a livelihood. The rustlers were Democrats, and devoted themselves to cattle stealing, murder, whisky and faro bank as steady pursuits. In those days Johnny Behan was sheriff of Cochise county and Virgil Earp was the marshal of Tombstone....

Barshall Williams [Marshal Williams] was then Wells Fargo agent at Tombstone, and when big money went out on the stage he tipped it off to Earp. The hold-ups were then planned in a convenient canyon. When the stage came along, at the word "Hands up!" Warren Earp, who was a stage company guard, meekly put his hands over his head. Then the hold-ups went through the express pouches and boxes like the grace of heaven through a camp meeting.

But it all came out on them. Williams, the Wells Fargo agent, confessed. It happened thus: It was a gala occasion in the Bird Cage opera house, in Tombstone. Sheriff Behan, Ike Clanton, Ringo and others of the cow thieves had boxes on one side. The Earps, Curley Bill [this is an interesting switch of allegiance], Doc Holliday, Nixon and others of the stage robbers, had boxes opposite. When one side cheered a performer, the others hissed, and as whisky flowed the spirits of both gangs mounted.

At last Ike Clanton took umbrage because Nixon, opposite, reposed his boot on the rail of his box. Clanton was too far away for conversation, so in testimony of his condemnation of Nixon's action he pulled his gun and put a bullet through Nixon's offensive foot. It came off the box rail.

Enthusiastic Shooting

Much good and enthusiastic shooting ensued. Twelve men were killed and wounded [complete nonsense]; none of the Earps, however. Williams, the confederate of Virgil and Wyatt Earp in the stage robbing, was badly shot up. He expected to die, and confessed. At this Wyatt Earp and his three brothers with others of their gang, fortified themselves in an old doby [adobe] house on the edge of Tombstone. Behan and the cow thieves put in what time they could spare from faro bank and theft to besieging them. The seige was a stand-off. At last Warren Earp—the foolhardy one—heeled himself and came down from

A FEAST OF GUNS
Wyatt as drawn by a cartoonist for The Artic Weekly Sun *August 5, 1900*

(Left to right) Ed Englestadt, Wyatt Earp and John Clum on the beach at Nome, 1900. Wyatt looks like he has just read the Seattle-Post *article on these pages. (JEFF MOREY COLLECTION)*

the doby fortress to play faro bank. He had just set a stack of blues on the king open when a cow thief listlessly put a bullet through his head.

Thus died the first of the Earps. There was more fighting then, and at last, the Earps were driven out of Tombstone and into the Gunnison [Colorado]. Their sister Jessy went with them [The Earps had no sister named Jessy—perhaps this refers to Hattie Ketchum, James Earp's step-daughter and a niece of Wyatt's, who some say had a thing for Tom McLaury]. Ike Clanton, one of the Democrats and cow thieves, followed them to Colorado and eloped with Jessy. This was too much for the Republican stage-robbing blood of Wyatt Earp and his brothers. They pursued. They ran Clanton and his bride into a mine tunnel. The miners interfered. There must be fair play. Ike Clanton offered to fight Virgil, Wyatt or Julian [Morgan?] Earp for their sister. Julian took it up. The two shot it out with pistols, and Julian was killed.

Thus died the second Earp. Ike

Clanton and Jessy, nee Earp, lived in peace two years [like Wyatt would let Ike go after he shot "Julian"]. Then Wyatt Earp, Virgil Earp and Curley Bill crossed up with Clanton, and there was another feast of guns. Clanton was killed, and took with him Curley Bill to the happy hunting grounds [this implies that Ike shot and killed "Curley Bill" Wow!] Wyatt Earp, when the smoke blew away, was also full of well made bullet holes, but he got well [Wyatt was never wounded].

The Third Earp Goes

And now the third Earp has passed in his checks, and in accordance with family traditions the coroner pulled off his boots. John Boyett [they actually got his name right!], a cowboy, evened a grudge of long standing over old rustler days by getting the drop on him and filling him full of lead.

It was only a few days before this that Earp met Boyett and, pressing a six-shooter against his stomach, took occasion to make insulting remarks about his ancestry, his daily occupa-

tion and his future prospects [nice piece of writing]. Boyett had to take it, but later his turn came and he added the fourth notch to his gun by killing Earp in a saloon as stated.

Wyatt Earp, the survivor of the quartette, is now 50 years old. He is grim, game and deadly. He never took water. But he doesn't kill as he used to. Age has cooled his blood, many wounds have brought him caution. Moreover, the communities he honors with his presence won't stand those gayeties which marked Wyatt Earp's earlier career. And Wyatt has grown to like a quiet life. As a result he has not taken a scalp in many years.

At one time when arrested for carrying a gun, Wyatt made this naive confession to the justice:

"Please your honor, force of habit is hard to overcome. I would as soon think of going without my shoes or my trousers as without my gun."

But while it is true that Mr. Wyatt Earp has not taken a scalp for years, those who know him best say that it is only for lack of sufficient provocation. During his residence in Seattle, he was one of the most quiet citizens, but it is not of record that any bluff was put up against him that went uncalled. It is known that in an unostentatious manner he promptly and severely rebuked the few attempts made to hand him what is technically known as the "con," and his manner was always such as to instill a wholesome respect in the minds of his immediate associates.

New Wyatt Research Surfaces

Researcher Carl Chafin has been transcribing George Parsons' journal for the past twenty-five years. Because Parsons' handwriting is so cramped and small, Chafin can only do several entries at a setting. Originally Chafin was only going to transcribe the seven years Parsons was in Tombstone, but then he realized that Wyatt and other Tombstoners show up in his later diary entries (he kept a faithful journal for the next 45 years ending in 1929). Carl has done thirty of the years one painful page at a time. The final manuscript "The West of George Whitwell Parsons" will include two million words. "Sometimes you agonize over one word for over a half hour," Chafin said from his home in California. "George wrote very small. It's hard to believe anyone could write that small." Last year, Chafin discovered Parsons' diary entries from Nome, Alaska.

Dated 1900, the entries cast new light on the exact whereabouts of Wyatt Earp. They also prove conclusively that he could not have come back to Willcox and avenged his brother Warren's death as some believe. Here, for the first time ever published are the new George Parsons' entries:

Wednesday, July 25, 1900

"Meeting friends constantly-Earp, ect. lively camp. No night."

Monday, August 27, 1900

"John Clum introduced me to

"The 'truth' about Wyatt Earp has roughly the same status as the 'truth' about King Arthur."
—TERRENCE RAFFERTY,
REVIEWER FOR THE *NEW YORKER*

WYATT'S "BABY PONY"

A photo of Wyatt's .41 caliber Single Action Army Colt revolver. Josephine Marcus Earp gave this pistol to Lincoln Ellsworth on September 11, 1937. She claimed that Wyatt called the gun "Baby Pony." The serial number is #87145 and it was manufactured in 1883 which puts it out of the time frame of the Tombstone events. *(JEFF MOREY COLLECTION)*

Knows Drink Evil So Backs Smith

Wyatt Earp, California pioneer who has been a republican in 60 years of voting, intends to mark his ballot for Al Smith this year.

By PEGGY BALLARD

THE "wild" days before prohibition were not as bad as the present ones, according to Wyatt Earp, California pioneer who has lived through the adventurous times of the west when it was the old west.

And, believing that Al Smith can change matters ofr the better, Earp is all for Al.

In 60 years of voting at presidential elections, Earp's only democratic vote was for Cleveland years ago. His second democratic vote will be cast for Al Smith, he said.

And he's so anxious to vote for Smith that he has postponed his winter trip to his mines in the mountains near San Bernardino until after Nov. 6.

Earp has been keeping up with politics and the progress of the west since he first came out to California from Iowa in 1864 via the covered wagon.

He was one of the early settlers in California in the helliroarin' old days. He drove a stage from San Bernardino to Los Angeles in '65 when bandits were at large, but his stage was never held up.

In '67 and '68 he was a freighter from Los Angeles to Salt Lake City and later on the trail from San Bernardino to Prescott.

Now and then there were a few mix-ups with Indians. Earp has his clothes shot to ribbons at times but he was never wounded.

Just before the big boom at Tombstone, Arizona, Earp ventured that way as a miner. Later he became a deputy sheriff and worked as police officer at other times at Wichita and Dodge City, Kansas.

During the Alaska gold rush he was in Wrangell. In attempting to go to Dawson, he was frozen in at Ramport.

Rex Beach played the banjo for the town dances then and brought the first mail in from Dawson, he remembers.

Since those days Earp has continued an active life, working his mines in the winters and summering in Los Angeles.

"My father lived to be 96 years of age and he always kept liquor in his house. That's a better way than this prohibition business which results in just as much liquor traffic but much worse liquor," Earp said.

At the age of 81 he is actively interested in the election and hoping urgently that Al Smith will be elected.

HAUGER OPENS NEW MEN'S STORE HERE

The Los Angeles Record October 19, 1928

his friend Englestadt tonight at Earp's place and he sang 'Jerusalem' with soprano and another woman accompanist. Strange sight—Earp dealing faro in corner, rough miners standing and some joining in chorus. Strange mixture."

Thursday, August 30, 1900
"John Clum, Fowler and I had an oldtimer with Wyatt Earp tonight at his place, a regular old Arizona time, and Wyatt unlimbered for several hours and seemed glad to talk to us who knew the past. It was a very memorable evening. He went home with us."

Friday, August 31, 1900
"We had such a seance last night. That evening with Wyatt Earp would have been worth $1,000 or more to the papers."

Friday, September 7, 1900
"With Clum and Earp awhile tonight. John goes out on 'St. Paul' [steamer]. Witnessed Earp's and Clum's stories signatory."

Saturday, September 8, 1900
"Saw Clum at his room awhile. The signatures I witnessed last night or tonight, I don't distinctly remember which, are to Earp's account of his adventures."

Monday, September 10, 1900
"Wyatt Earp and I had a little confab today. This reputed bad man from Arizona is straight and fearless I believe. And is a good friend of mine and respects me and I him, even though he runs perhaps the biggest drinking and gambling places here. It's well to have such a friend here and let the thugs see it."

Wild Times With The Truth
Virtually all the efforts of the current century to "get it right" when it comes to the Wyatt Earp story have produced an avalanche

of criticism from the numerous Earp researchers and self-appointed experts. Listening to them, nobody to this day has come close to getting it right (of course when they come out with their book, all that will change). This book you are holding in your hands is no exception. Although every effort possible went into achieving complete accuracy, a noted Tombstone expert, Carl Chafin, has dismissed the book as having "a mistake on every page." And so it goes.

With that said, let's nit pick the recent big-budget movies, "Tombstone" and "Wyatt Earp."

What's Right in "Wyatt Earp"

• It is long and enough time is taken to cover Wyatt's eventful early years.

• This is the only film to show all five of the Earp brothers: James, Virgil, Wyatt, Morgan and Warren.

• Peripheral figures in Wyatt's life are featured; Ed Masterson, Mike Meagher, Larry Deger, are usually ignored in Westerns. For the historically minded, these appearances are a real treat. Also, while they don't appear, it's nice to hear Bob Paul's and Budd Philpot's names mentioned.

• Significant lines in the film are from the historical record. For example, when Wyatt Earp says to Ike Clanton, "You talk too much for a fighting man." Source: Lake's book, page 281. Wyatt tells Johnny Behan, "Johnny, if your not careful, you'll see me once too often." This line, or a form of it, appears throughout Earp literature. The first book to make mention of it, was Alfred Henry Lewis' "The Sunset Trail" published in 1905, page 356.

• For once, Wyatt is properly identified as a deputy marshal of

THE TOWN TOO EXPENSIVE TO DIE

Consider this: "Wyatt Earp" and "Tombstone" spent a combined budget of $100 million dollars to film two movies. That figure is more than all the silver profits ever taken out of the ground in the entire history of Tombstone. "Wyatt Earp" spent $6.5 million reproducing Tombstone on a cold knoll south of Santa Fe. (A rumor in Tombstone says that Costner approached the town council about filming in the actual Tombstone and wanted their blessing to restore it to its original look. The council allegedly split and eventually said no because they didn't want Hollywood monkeying with their historical buildings. The irony is that most of the buildings in Tombstone date from the twenties and thirties.) Both movies do a commendable job with the look of Tombstone. Since the movies have come out, tourism has increased to 300,000 visitors a season.

Fly's Boarding House & Photo Gallery does not appear to have been built yet

The Harwood house and site of the gunfight

TOMBSTONE, 1880 (ARIZONA HISTORICAL SOCIETY)

"What kind of town is this, anyhow?"
—HENRY FONDA AS WYATT EARP IN
"MY DARLING CLEMENTINE"

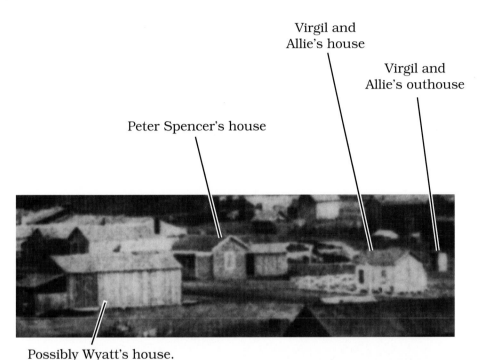

Virgil and
Allie's house

Virgil and
Allie's outhouse

Peter Spencer's house

Possibly Wyatt's house.
We're not exactly sure
when he occupied this lot.

Dodge City (he was never the marshal).

• The shooting of Ed Masterson by Alf Walker and Jack Wagner is depicted pretty much as Dodge City newspapers reported it.

• The buffalo hunting camp is beautifully mounted. For once the hunters aren't all presented as hulking neanderthals (The negative buffalo hunter stereotype, as portrayed in the media, has never received proper attention from the A.C.L.U.).

• In 1882 the train didn't go to Tombstone. So when Morgan's body is shipped to California, the film properly shows the Contention City depot.

• The film has a remarkably well-balanced portrayal of Johnny Behan. Rather than being presented as a petty little fixer, Behan is pictured as a flexible realist.

What's Wrong With "Wyatt Earp"
• How can a three hour movie not have enough time to define the major antagonists—the cow-boys? The cow-boys aren't well-defined characters but mere background figures.

• The costuming is painfully inadequate. Costner's black hat is circa 1920s. Wyatt wears a 1950s style buscadero holster. The cow-boys all dress in blacks and browns. Where are the colorful outfits that led Oscar Wilde to compare cow-boys to pirates of old? Ike Clanton acts and dresses like a New York wino. Is that a hat he's wearing or a lampshade? The cow-boys wear bat-wing chaps, a style that didn't become popular until well after 1900.

• Where is Johnny Ringo—on the cutting room floor?

• Period detail is sometimes from the wrong period. When Wyatt meets Doc Holliday, we see a contemporary—make that 1990s—U.S. Cavalry flag hanging on display. Where is the Twilight Zone theme when you need it?

Logan Clark (above) of Phelan, California, poses with his horse Rustle on the set of "Tombstone." Logan is a member of the "Buckaroos," a reenactment group that was paid $750 a week ($300 for the horse) to camp out on location and be in the movie. When the film crew finished for the day and headed back to Tucson for the night, Logan and the Buckaroos camped out in tents and waited for the crew to return in the morning. Thirty of them did this for three and a half months. Obviously, part of the "authentic" look in the movie is the genuine crustiness of the cow-boy extras. As to the competition, Logan falls into the Stickler for Detail Camp, "I won't go see 'Wyatt Earp' because Kevin Costner wears a Buscadero rig with a buckle on it."

Kirk Douglas (left) as Doc Holliday confronts Ike Clanton in "Gunfight at the O.K. Corral," 1957

• In an early scene around the dinner table we meet the Earp family. Sitting with the group is Wyatt's older sister Martha—age 18. Unfortunately, Martha Earp, who was born on Sept. 25, 1845, died on May 26, 1856, age ten

DID THE COW-BOYS REALLY WEAR RED SASHES LIKE THEY DO IN THE MOVIE "TOMBSTONE"?

Charles M. Bruce displays a tie, a bandanna and a sash. C.S. Fly photo, Tombstone, A.T., 1887. (Arizona Historical Society)

Fly's Gallery,   Tombstone, A. T.

Cow-Boy Gang Bangers

In the John Pleasant Gray memoirs (written in the forties and on file at the Arizona Historical Society), Gray claims that Billy Leonard, one of the alleged Benson stage robbers, had a biography of Wild Bill Hickok and that all his cow-boy cronies were taken with Hickok and his style of dress—which sometimes included a sash. Screenwriter Kevin Jarre made a leap of imagination and came up with a modern connection; gang colors and bandannas, which are worn for identification and solidarity.

THE BOOK THAT STARTED IT ALL

Stuart Lake's tome to Wyatt Earp, (right), came out in 1931 and has been the fodder for numerous movies. Costner's "Wyatt Earp" borrowed heavily from its pages. Notice anything wrong in the cover painting? Pssst. There's only three in the Earp party, Doc is missing.

years-eight months and one day.

• All the Kansas scenes were filmed in the winter. The cow-boys wear heavy coats and breathe steamy breath. However, in real life, the herds came to the cowtowns only during the summer months, making these scenes seem odd and out of joint.

• Why doesn't Curly Bill have curly hair? He looks like he goes to Don King's barber.

• While the Earp wives are well-defined, the cow-boys aren't. From some of the scenes one would expect the climactic shootout to be between Wyatt and his sisters-in-law.

> *"Ahead, Iron Springs was hidden by an eroded bank possibly fifteen feet high. Beyond the hollow, where the mountain slope resumed, was a grove of cottonwoods."*
> —STUART LAKE,
> DESCRIBING WYATT EARP'S APPROACH TO IRON SPRINGS IN "FRONTIER MARSHAL"

Reality—Where Fiction Meets the Road

The actual approach, (above left) and springs (above right), where Wyatt Earp allegedly shot Curly Bill.

In the movie "Tombstone" Iron Springs (today called Mescal Springs) becomes a lush pond where Wyatt wades in and kills Curly Bill. In "Wyatt Earp," Costner is framed by high canyon walls. As you can see in the photos above, the approach and the springs do not match the fiction.

HUGH O'BRIAN RIDES AGAIN

In the wake of all the Earp fever, Hugh O'Brian revived his role as Wyatt Earp in the CBS TV movie, "Wyatt Earp: Return to Tombstone", which aired July 2, 1994 and featured an aging Wyatt riding into town in a horseless carriage. Today, Hugh helps kids through the Hugh O'Brian Youth Foundation (HOBY). He did quite well with the original series (earning $3,000 a week) and he invested wisely, "I don't have to touch my principal or principles."

• The ship taking Wyatt and Josephine to Alaska seems to have two names. In a long shot we clearly see the name "Spirit of '98" on the bow of the vessel. In the next shot we see a smokestack with the name "City of Seattle" emblazoned on it. (Check your tickets please!) For some inexplicable reason Johnny-behind-the-duece is called Tommy-behind-the-duece. Go figure.

• In the movie, Virgil Earp is shot in the right arm whereas the real Virgil was shot in the left arm. In the movie, Tom McLaury is shot in the left side whereas the real Tom was shot in the right side by Doc Holliday's shotgun. Holliday, on the other hand, was never knocked off his feet at the O.K. Corral gunfight as the film depicts.

• In both "Wyatt Earp" and "Tombstone" Frank McLaury is shot in the forehead. The real Frank, however, was hit under the right ear.

What's Right About "Tombstone"
• The costuming is the best replication of 1880's style outfitting since the films of De Mille.

• The town of Tombstone looks newly built and freshly painted— as it would have appeared in 1880.

• The Birdcage Theatre is reproduced beautifully.

• Virtually every name on every building refers to an actual business in Tombstone during the Earp era: The Can Can Restaurant, Sandy Bob's Stageline, J.V. Vickers Real Estate, Rockaway Oyster House, Dragoon Saloon, Key West Cigar Store, Andy's Club Saloon to name but a few.

"Why can't the Earps and the cow-boys just get along?"
—JEFF MOREY

TRUE GUNS
All of the weaponry in "Tombstone" was carefully picked to insure authenticity to the period. Wyatt carries a Steven's 10-gauge just as he is reported to have used. Virgil carries a Smith & Wesson #3 Russian as history indicates he did. Not long after the movie came out a gun dealer ran into Peter Sherayko, who plays Texas Jack in "Tombstone." The dealer commented that he had seen the film three times and still hadn't found an unauthentic weapon. "And you never will," replied Sherayko confidently.

"TOMBSTONE," 1993

"GUNFIGHT AT THE O.K. CORRAL," 1957

WALKIN' THAT WALK
"This is why we all wanted to do this film, isn't it?" Dennis Quaid is reported to have said when they started filming the walk to the gunfight for "Wyatt Earp." Each generation of Wyatt movies carries on the tradition of four men, walking side by side, even though history says they were bunched up, two in front and two in back.

• The use of period vernacular such as "It doesn't take much to get the budge on a dub like you," is the best in a movie since "True Grit."

• Much of the dialogue is from the historical record. When Fred White says "The Oriental is a regular slaughterhouse," the source is George Parson's journal, March 1, 1881. During the gunfight—when Frank McLaury says, "I've got you this time," Doc Holliday replies "You're a daisy if you do!"—this is a direct quote from the Tombstone *Nugget's* October 27, 1881, description of the shootout. When Johnny Ringo challenges the Earps to shoot it out—Doc Holliday steps in and says, "I'm your huckleberry—that's just my game." The source is Walter Noble Burns' "Tombstone," page 138.

• Tom McLaury wears a silver hatband at the gunfight. Testimony at the Spicer Hearing specifically notes that McLaury had a silver hatband.

• At the gunfight, Billy Clanton wears his gun cross-draw style, on his left hip. Once again, this is born out in the Spicer hearing.

• When Morgan Earp is murdered, the "barking dog" is from the *Nugget* account of the shooting.

What's Wrong With "Tombstone"
• The opening Mexican wedding scene has no bearing on any actual historical event in the Earp saga and appears to be part of the producer's and director Cosmotos' attempt to beef up the action quotient by copping a blatant Sam Pecinpah riff.

• When the Earps arrive in Tombstone in 1879 the Birdcage Theatre is already standing even though it won't be built until 1881.

"'Tombstone' rescues Wyatt Earp from villainy without trying to restore his halo."
—ALLEN BARRA,
THE VILLAGE VOICE

June 9, 1993

Jeff Morey, (above left), and Kevin Jarre sit on a hilltop overlooking "Rustler's Park" during the filming of "Tombstone" near Elgin, Arizona. (Ironically, the distant butte beyond Jarre's head is within sight of the actual spot where Wyatt Earp allegedly shot Curly Bill).

Morey was the historical consultant on the film and he helped writer-director Jarre ("Glory") unravel the complicated story and enigmatic character of Wyatt Earp. Jarre, in turn, spun out a masterful, and for the most part, historically accurate script. From the beginning of production the first time director insisted on using only authentic costumes, hats and weapons (A visitor to the set made Jarre beam with pride when he commented that the hats were the best he had ever seen in a movie).

It looked like Hollywood was finally going to make a bonafied, historically accurate movie about Wyatt Earp.

Unfortunately, two days after this photo was taken, Jarre was fired as director and replaced by "action" director George Cosmotos (he did one of the "Rambos"). An extensive rewrite of the script was ordered.

According to scuttlebutt on the set, Jarre was moving too slow and the camera wasn't moving fast enough (a reference to the producer's desire for a MTV driven camera style).

Almost a year after the release of "Tombstone" close friends say that Kevin Jarre has yet to see it.

Allie Earp, age 17 (photo courtesy of Red Marie's)

• Doc Holliday kills Ed Bailey in Prescott, A.T., but it really happened at Fort Griffin, Texas.

• Marshal Fred White is portrayed as an older man (this is true of almost every portrayal— Fred White *sounds* middleaged) when in fact he was only 31 when he was shot down by Curly Bill. And by the way, in real life, Wyatt Earp helped get Curly Bill off, when he testified at Curly's trial in Tucson that the shooting was an accident. He even demonstrated to the court how the gun could have accidently been fired.

• In history, when Doc Holliday converted to Catholicism on his deathbed, the priest who befriended him was Father Ed Downey. Screenwriter Kevin Jarre changed the priest's name in the movie to Father Feeney as a tribute to Director John Ford, whose father's name was Americanized from O'Fienne to Feeney.

• Doc Holliday died at the Hotel Glenwood, not in a sanitarium.

• When Wyatt and Josie visit Doc on his deathbed, Wyatt is carrying a booklet he wrote called "My Friend Doc Holliday" by Wyatt Earp. After the movie "Tombstone" came out in December of 1993, the Territorial Bookstore in Tombstone was besieged with tourists asking for the book by name. There was only one problem—there was no such book. But after 250 visitors asked for the non-existent book in a single weekend, capped off by an irate book buyer who accused clerk Jack Fisk of lying to cover up the fact he didn't have the book, Jack figured "why fight 'em." Fisk went out and printed a book called "My Friend Doc Holliday" by Wyatt Earp as told to Jack Fisk. He has sold hundreds.

"Law And Order" 1932

Stacy Keach as "Doc" 1971

Richard Dix in "Tombstone— The Town too Tough to Die" 1942

Henry Fonda, Linda Darnell and Victor Mature in "My Darling Clementine" 1947 (Below) James Garner and Jason Robards in "Hour Of The Gun" 1967

Val Kilmer, (left), as Doc and Kurt Russell as Wyatt Earp in "Tombstone." Russell wins the "Best Wyatt Mustache" award hands down. Although the word from the set is that Kurt showed up with even longer flowing mustaches, but the producers made him trim it back.

Wyatt Earp's actual signature.

The logo for Costner's "Wyatt Earp."

Author's Note

The reason there are photos in this section of every Wyatt Earp film *except* "Wyatt Earp" is this: Several days before going to press, the Warner Brothers' legal department called and refused to allow us to run any publicity photos from the film "Wyatt Earp," unless we paid them $250 per image *and* received written permission from Kevin Costner. Realizing that the latter was about as likely as getting a urine sample from Dennis Quaid, we removed the photos. We are very disappointed but realize that the legal department at Warner Brothers is probably afraid if we ran the photos somebody might actually want to see the film.

Dueling Docs

If there's one thing everybody agrees on regarding "Tombstone" and "Wyatt Earp" it's that Doc Holliday steals both movies.

Writing in the *Riverfront Times*, movie reviewer Allen Barra says "Thin, pale and red-eyed, [Val] Kilmer's Holliday seems to be sweating alcohol through his pores; he looks as if he has no soul left to trade with the devil. He's already given it to Edgar Allen Poe." Barra also believes that Kilmer was robbed of an Oscar for his portrayal of the deadly dentist. "Disney Studios, spooked by bad publicity when Jarre was fired, scarcely allowed any critics to advance-screen the movie," Barra asserts. Movie politics aside, most movie goers who have seen the surprise hit ($60,000,000 in the first ten months) wholeheartedly agree.

Meanwhile, at Cook's ranch south of Santa Fe, Dennis Quaid showed up for the filming of "Wyatt Earp" having lost 43 pounds. The normally one-hundred-and-eighty pound actor brought his own doctor (a doc to help him play Doc!) to help insure that he only looked sick. His wife, actress Meg Ryan, was reportedly very worried about his health, and rightfully so: In the movie Quaid looks like death warmed over, or, in other words—a dead on Doc.

After a sneak of the film in June an Earp buff who saw the three hour opus gushed, "I firmly believe that's as close as we'll ever get to seeing the real Doc Holliday actually walk and talk."

Unfortunately, not many movie viewers have seen Quaid's stunning performance because "Wyatt Earp" has managed to earn back only a fraction of it's cost.

The End of The Trail?

Somewhere, the two of them must be chuckling, or at least Wyatt is—Josie is probably having a conniption fit over her recent "scandalous" inclusion in the legend.

Around their final resting place south of San Francisco, the waves of curious visitors ebb and flow (At the peak of the fifties Earpamania, Wyatt's headstone was stolen). This phenomenon seems to have hit a generational rhythm that recycles itself every twenty years, with the inevitable onslaught of another avalanche of books and movies (finally getting to the Real Truth!).

As these things go, the hoopla is sure to fade again and the mania will wane.

But, as with all good legends, the end is only the beginning.

FROM ASHES TO ASHES

The current wave of Wyatt seekers leave coins, flowers and an occasional bullet on Wyatt's and Josie's graves in Colma, California. Wyatt was actually cremated in Los Angeles and then hand carried in an urn, by rail, by Josie to his final resting place. She likewise was cremated after her death and joined him in December of 1944. (photos by Dick George)

WYATT AND JOSIE

They met in Tombstone, and ended up together under one.

Special Thanks: to all the people who helped with this addendum— Jeff Morey, for his thoughts, photos and words. Carl Chafin, for allowing the use of his hard won journal entries from George Parsons (and thanks to ol' George who went to the trouble of writing it down in the first place!). Also, thanks to Dave Ritter for all the late hours and talent. Thanks to Theresa and all the gang at Tri Star. Thanks to Eddie Brandt Photos for the old Wyatt movie stills, and to Robert Burton for his marketing insight. Additional thanks to Jim Dunham, Allen Barra and Dick George.